KU-407-436

Non fiction Gift Aid

£

0 031140 002258

The Chief

The Chief

The life story of
Robert Baden-Powell

Eileen K. Wade

**Foreword by Sir William
Gladstone, Bt., Chief Scout
of the United Kingdom and
Overseas Branches**

Wolfe

This revised edition
published 1975 by
Wolfe Publishing Limited
10 Earlham Street
London WC2H 9LP

© Eileen K. Wade 1975

Hardback edition SBN 7234 0631 6
Paperback edition SBN 7234 0679 0

Printed in Great Britain by
Ebenezer Baylis and Son Limited,
The Trinity Press, Worcester, and London

First published 1924 under the
title *The Piper of Pax* by
C. Arthur Pearson Ltd

Contents

Illustrations

Between pages 80 and 81

7

All the photographs were selected from the files in the Publicity Department at The Scout Association. We are grateful to the Department for their kind co-operation. Copyright to all photographs, except the following, is owned by The Scout Association. Number 13, source unknown; 18, Topix; 19, Photo by 'Tell'; 22, source unknown; 23, Kendricks; 25, 26 and 28, source unknown; 29, Universal Pictorial Press and Agency; 30, Keystone Press; 31, Sport and General; 32, Bureau of Information, Kenya.

Jacket photograph supplied by Handford Photography.

Author's Note

This book was written over fifty years ago when I was in daily touch with B-P and was able to check the manuscript with the help of his pencilled notes which I still possess.

I have slightly amended, and added to, the original book to bring it up to date for present-day readers, but the material which B-P saw and approved is still there.

I should like to thank Rex Hazlewood for his help, and many suggestions in the rewriting of this story of B-P with whom I worked so happily for twenty-seven years.

EKW

Foreword

Throughout human history, there has been a small company of men and women of different nations and of various professions whose lives and actions, ideas and ideals have enriched the world and added to the happiness of mankind. I do not doubt that among these Robert Stephenson Smyth Baden-Powell must be included.

Although his original training methods and his exploits in India and South Africa and elsewhere (which these pages recall) had already made his name familiar to many of his fellow army officers, it was his high-spirited defence of the little town of Mafeking during the Boer War which made his name a household word. He was a national hero, but particularly and understandably he was the hero of the British boys of that time, which was the early years of our present century. So when his book *Scouting for Boys* appeared in 1908, the author was no stranger to the boys concerned. Here in these 'yarns', as the chapters were called, were interesting things to be learnt and exciting things to do. Soon all over the country (and before long in other countries, too) boys were putting up their tents, cooking their meals over wood fires, learning to fend for themselves and using their eyes as they had never used them before. They were Scouts and he was their Chief.

I suppose to today's Scouts, Baden-Powell is just an historical figure, even if, to them, rather a special one. But among older folk, there will still be alive many who saw him, listened to him or knew him well: there will remain just a few who knew him very well indeed. And of these not many can have known B–P as well as the lady who is the author of this book. Mrs Wade (or Miss Eileen Nugent as she then was) had been for some months a member of the staff of the Boy Scout Headquarters, then situated in Victoria

Street, Westminster, when one Sunday morning in 1914, she was asked to go to 32 Princes Gate, Kensington where the Chief Scout and Lady Baden-Powell were living, to take down some letters. Thereafter she remained B–P's confidential secretary until he left England in 1938.

Anything written or edited by Mrs Wade about B–P therefore carries the stamp of an original, contemporary and personal documentary source of history. This book of hers which was first published some years ago, now appears again with revisions. How fortunate for us that it does.

I am sure that it will be widely read, much enjoyed and long remembered. There would have been no Scouts, no Guides, today, if B–P had not been the great and unique man he was—and here he is portrayed and recalled for us by someone who knew him well over so many years.

Sir William Gladstone, Bt.,
Chief Scout of the United Kingdom and Overseas Branches

To the Scouts of today

Into the street the piper stepped,
Smiling first a little smile,
As if he knew what magic slept
In his quiet pipe the while.

And the piper advanced
And the children followed.

Robert Browning

1 London

To the heart of youth
The world is a highwayside.

Robert Louis Stevenson

In a quiet street, then known as Stanhope Street, on the north side of Hyde Park, there was born on 22nd February 1857 a boy whose future career was destined to have very wide reaching effects.

Robert Stephenson Smyth Baden-Powell, 1st Baron, OM, GCVO, GCMG, KCB, FRGS, DCL, LLD, the Founder of the Scout Movement, was the sixth son and the eighth of ten children of the Rev. Professor Baden Powell by his third wife, Henrietta Grace.

Baden Powell (Baden was his Christian name) came from a long line of gentlemen farmers and merchants, but from his boyhood he had wished to become a clergyman. He was a clever boy who became a learned man. After some years as a curate (of Midhurst in Sussex) and then as a vicar (of Plumstead in Kent) he accepted the University of Oxford's offer of The Chair of Geometry and so became a professor of mathematics. His intellectual interests were wide-ranging, but particularly educational, scientific and philosophical. He was a member of the Royal Commission of 1850 which widened the scope of university's curriculum and was a contributor to a book of essays concerned with Christianity and science, called *Essays and Reviews*, which created a great stir in its day.

But all his life he remained true to his Christian faith in his way of living and in his preaching and teaching. He was a friend of the leading authors and scientists of his day.

17

In his memoirs fifty years after his father's death, B-P said:

I had a peculiar father, a man of striking personality. He just breathed Love. He had a brain which placed him in the front rank of scientists whether in astronomy, geology, chemistry or light. He was at the same time a leader among the students of theology, a good writer and a fluent speaker. Yet he liked the life of a country parson and was very fond of children.

Mrs Baden Powell (the name was later hyphenated) was the daughter of Admiral W. H. Smyth, DCL, FRS, and sister of Professor Piazzi Smyth, the then Astronomer Royal for Scotland. Scouts and Guides throughout the world have more to thank her for than perhaps they will ever know, for, as B-P often said, it was largely due to her encouragement and belief in its possibilities that the Boy Scout Movement ever made its start in the world.

She brought up five sons and was, with Miss Shirreff and Mrs Grey, one of the original pioneers of the Girls' Public High Schools in Great Britain. She liked to think that her family was connected with the adventurous Captain John Smith, the founder of Virginia. Actually no descent can be traced, although one of his best-known sayings seems specially applicable to B-P, who often used to quote it to his Scouts: 'We are born not for ourselves but to do good unto others.'

It will be seen that, if heredity counts for anything, the young Baden-Powells had a good start in life although the widowed mother was hard put to it to find the money necessary for the upbringing and education of her large family.

Happy is the childhood—like the nation—which has no history, and there were few events in the first few years of B-P's life which could usefully be set down in print.

He was born into a London of crinolines and horses: a London into which Selfridges and cinemas, Aldwych and Kingsway, cars and motor-buses, had yet to find their way.

His godfather, from whom he took his first two names, was Robert Stephenson, the celebrated civil engineer and builder of bridges.

Mrs Baden-Powell had the advantage of friendship with many

of the most eminent scholars, writers, and artists of her day and she was not above asking their advice in the education of her children.

Thus the author John Ruskin found the future Chief Scout as a small boy drawing with his right and left hands alternately, and advised his mother to let him continue the practice—one which stood him in good stead in all his after life as regards writing, drawing and modelling.

The distinguished novelist William Makepeace Thackeray was also a frequent visitor and B-P used to treasure a shilling presented to him by the great man. It was on the occasion of a dinner party at his mother's house that B-P took the opportunity of escaping from the night nursery and joining the circle of guests, clad only in his night-dress. Thackeray, evidently fearing a scene, bribed him with a shilling to make himself scarce before his presence should be discovered by the authorities.

When he was about three his father died and the family moved from Stanhope Street to Hyde Park Gate South, and here was spent the greater part of B-P's early childhood. He was educated mainly at home by his mother, though for a short time he attended a Dame's School in Kensington Square. He could never remember learning anything there but remembered that he wore, at that period, a pork-pie hat which had an upturned brim and that as he was running to school one wet day with his brim filled with rain water, a butcher-boy coming round the corner, seized it from his head and shook it over the already partially drowned rat.

Until his grandfather, Admiral Smyth, died in 1865, B-P wrote regularly to him and it was in this year too that he carefully composed:

'Laws for me when I am old. I will have the poor people to be as rich as we are, and they ought by rights to be as happy as we are, and all who go across the crossings shall give the poor crossing sweepers some money and you ought to thank God for what he has given us and He has made the poor people to be poor and the rich people to be rich, and I can tell you how to be good, now I will tell you. You must pray to God whenever you can but you cannot be good with only praying but you must also try very hard to be good. By R. S. S. Powell.'

The boy was indeed 'father to the man'.

So at a very early age B-P displayed the characteristics, the energy, ambidexterity and versatility which distinguished him in his later life. With his family of brothers he learned to work intelligently, to pick up knowledge, to camp and fend for himself, to manage a boat and to play games—or, as it might be summed up, to 'scout'.

At the age of eleven B-P was sent to a preparatory school, Rose Hill, at Tunbridge Wells, under a Mr Allfrey. Here he won a great tribute from his headmaster who, when the boy left, told his mother that he would gladly have kept him on without fees of any kind, so great was his influence on the moral tone of the school.

But the boy had made good use of his time and had won an entrance scholarship to Fettes School, where he would no doubt have gone had he not at the same time secured an entrance to Charterhouse as a gown boy foundationer, on the nomination of the Duke of Marlborough. The old Charterhouse was in London, and so was much nearer home than Edinburgh—and to Charterhouse he accordingly went in 1870.

The first term at a public school can never have the same horrors for a boy who has lived among four brothers at home as it can have for an only child. No prefect could have been sterner with the boys under his care than was B-P's oldest brother Warington who, from his pinnacle in the Navy, instructed his younger brothers in the arts of seamanship and no doubt in other more important matters as well.

The following incident, told in B-P's own words, will show that life under Warington's command was not all beer and skittles:

'Frank will sit by and see that you eat the whole of that muck yourself,' was the verdict pronounced on me by my eldest brother. By virtue of being a sailor he was the captain of our crew. We four brothers manned a five-ton cutter and had the time of our lives cruising round the coast of England and Scotland in her.

But this was my first voyage and being the youngest I had been unanimously elected cabin boy and cook and—more especially—washer-up. My first attempt at pea soup had proved something of a failure owing partly to a smoking fire and scalded pot and that sort of thing, and partly to the fact that I had not realised that some form of meaty ingredient was desirable and that more water than meal was usual in compounding a soup.

Hence the above verdict. But in such a school and under such a master I pretty soon learned not only how to cook but also to 'hand reef and steer whatever the emergency'—and our emergencies were many and varied. To this day I don't know how we all came out of it alive; but to this day also the lessons then learned have stood me in good stead on many a difficult occasion.

2 Charterhouse

The men that tanned the hide of us,
Our daily foes and friends,
They shall not lose their pride of us
Howe'er the journey ends.

Henry Newbolt

Charterhouse, in Smithfield in the city of London, was a very venerable building when B-P entered it at the age of thirteen.

Dr Haig-Brown had been appointed its headmaster in 1863 and it was under his care that the whole of B-P's Charterhouse days were spent. He was described as the 'strong type' of headmaster, a man who inspired masters and scholars alike with profound respect. In his book *Indian Memories* B-P told a story which shows that the Doctor also possessed a sense of humour and some sympathy with boyish escapades:

The fight between the butcher boys of the neighbouring Smithfield Market and the boys of Charterhouse had become a standing institution and very often these battles raged for days together. On this particular occasion the Smithfield boys had taken possession of a waste piece of ground 'Over Hoardings', adjoining our football ground from which they attacked us with showers of stones and brickbats whenever we attempted to play. This was responded to from our side in like manner, with occasional sorties of strong bodies of us over the wall. With four or five other boys, too small to take part in the actual fray, I was looking on at the battle when we suddenly found the headmaster alongside us, anxiously watching the progress of the fight. He remarked to us—'I think if you boys went through that door in the side wall you might attack them in flank.'

'Yes Sir,' one of us replied, 'but the door is locked.'
The worthy doctor fumbled in his gown and said 'That is so, but here is the key.'
He sent us on our way rejoicing, and our attack was a complete success.

Dr Haig-Brown had not been long at Charterhouse before he realised that, if the school were to grow and expand on a scale worthy of its foundation and traditions, it must leave the crowded quarters of the City and make a fresh start in the country. Though there was at first great opposition from the authorities, he persuaded them in the end to buy a site at Godalming and on it to build the school that is now known as Charterhouse to thousands of boys, and Old Boys.

The decision to move had in fact been made in 1867, three years before B-P joined the school, but it was not until 1872 that the move was actually completed. So that during the whole of B-P's school days upheaval and transition were in the air.

The following words of Dr Haig-Brown will show how even quite a young boy can help in a situation of this kind. Speaking of B-P he said:

In the somewhat trying circumstances of this removal he proved most useful. He showed remarkable intelligence and liberality of feeling— most boys are so conservative by nature—helping to smooth over the difficulties involved in the change to a new place and taking up every school institution which was new. He was by nature a born leader of boys as he has since become of men.

These words were spoken in 1900 when the world was ringing with the story of the defence of Mafeking. After that time the 'leader of men' returned to his earlier occupation, the leadership of boys. Dr Haig-Brown never lived to see the fulfilment of his former pupil's greatest work, the creation of the Boy Scout Movement.

A contemporary of B-P's at the old Charterhouse gives the following picture of him:

Into this house (Gownboys) and this well-ordered, high-spirited and on the whole very happy community, entered the future Chief Scout at the age of thirteen, a boy of medium size, curly red hair, decidedly freckled, with a pair of twinkling eyes that soon won friends for him. It is possible that he did not altogether enjoy his new life at first as the ways of his new world were rather strange to him: he no doubt had his share of undeserved blows and kicks, and it took him a little time to fall into the ways of his companions. As a fag he was beyond all praise. His upper, or fag-master, for whom it was his duty to prepare toast, etc. for breakfast and supper, was often served by him with extra delicacies which we have every reason to believe were the fruits of that Scouting spirit which he afterwards developed for an even greater purpose. He might then have been seen on any evening after six, one of a group of heated boys in front of the big writing-school fire, struggling to keep his toasting fork in a good place, exchanging winged words with his rivals and thoroughly enjoying his experiments in the culinary art, learning tricks which were to be useful to him later on in many parts of the world.

He was always cheerful, perfectly straight and clean in every way; with nothing whatever of the prig about him he tacitly discouraged all vulgar swearing and evil talking, and was certainly an influence for good all through his school life. At the same time he was always rather unlike other boys, who were often puzzled by him, and never quite knew when he was joking and when he was serious. Generally popular, he never seemed to make any very close friends, and the prestige he gradually acquired arose from his good-humour, his powers of mimicry and his many quaint antics which to the ordinary boy marked him out as being gifted with an admirable species of madness.

The progress of B-P from the bottom to the top of his school has been described as steady rather than brilliant. It was not always very steady. His reports contained such remarks as 'Classics: he seems to take very little interest in his work', or 'Mathematics: has to all intents given up the study of mathematics'. But he was the type of clever, talented, many-sided boy whose outward progress is misleading as his easy rise to the top in Charterhouse and his later career shows. Neither over-studious nor a games fanatic, he was a good all-round worker and player, with so many irons in the fire that he never had any idle time on his hands. He played all the games that were going and distinguished himself at football, winning his way into the School XI in his last year. 'A good goal-keeper, always keeping very cool,' reported the School magazine of 1876. He was in the Cadet Corps and Rifle team and is reported to have shot the only bull's eye that was scored in the Public Schools match at Wimbledon in 1874.

Like most other boys B-P was better at some lessons than others but he reached the sixth form with comparative ease.

He confessed to a dislike for mathematics and classics, but characteristically made the best of a bad job. 'A good many things appealed to me when I was at school,' he wrote later, 'in fact I really think that most things appealed in their way. But Greek just didn't happen to be one of them. I hated Greek. I know it sounds immoral, but there is no use making any pretence about it. I just hated it. This went on right up to my last term at school and then, late in the day it is true, but better late than never, Mr T. E. Page gave me quite a new outlook on the language by demon-strating the dramatic possibilities and beauties that underlay the tangle of aorists and accents.'

Dramatic possibilities: here was the silver lining to the cloud. B-P was a born actor and in the school dramatic performance he made a reputation which never deserted him throughout his subse-quent career. Not only did he find the greatest amusement in it himself but in many a tight place was able to help his friends by the exercise of his dramatic abilities.

Dr Haig-Brown used to recall how on one occasion, at a school entertainment, a promised performer failed to put in an appear-ance. The boys were getting rather impatient so the Doctor turned to B-P, sitting near to him, and asked if he could do anything to fill the gap.

Without turning a hair the boy rose, got on to the stage and began to recount some episodes of school life, keeping the other boys in roars of laughter with his take-off of a French lesson. Fortunately the French master was not present!

As a clown, a pianist, a fiddler, and most especially as a comic artist, B-P, or Bathing-Towel as the school called him, was in constant demand. And when he had any time on his hands he used to take lessons in brick-laying and mortar mixing from the builders employed on the school chapel and, incidentally, to make friends with the men themselves and learn something of their homes and surroundings.

In 1878 he had reached the top of the school and was made a monitor, and the description which the headmaster gave of his services in this capacity at that time is just the description which would apply to the best sort of Patrol Leader today:

'*The duties of his responsible position he discharged with judgment and fidelity. Loyally attached to the traditions of the school, he brought his intelligence to bear on their interpretation. In his attitude to the younger boys he was generous, kind and encouraging.*'

It is not everyone who has the luck to be born with so many talents but on the other hand talents are not much use if, like the gentleman in the parable, you go and bury them. B-P always made the most of his many and various gifts while at school, and among these was a good voice for singing.

Here is his own description, written some years later, of his initiation into the choir:

When I first went to my public school, Charterhouse, the celebrated John Hullah was the music master. He took us new boys into the beautiful old tapestried room at the Charterhouse—the room in which Queen Elizabeth had often been—and there he tried our voices. Each boy, after being tested, was sent to one or other corner of the room. When it came to my turn I was put into a third corner, all by myself, and there I remained, the solitary one, until all the boys present had been tried.

It turned out later that one lot were likely singers for the choir, the other lot had either no voice or no ear, while I—poor me—was judged to have a falsetto voice. How Mr Hullah discovered this as I was only then a shrill treble, I don't know, but it was quite true for I was shoved into the choir and there I remained for six years. When my talking voice 'broke' I was still able to sing and by the end of my time at school I was able to take any part needed, whether soprano, alto, tenor or baritone.

I don't say that I had a good voice in any of them, for I certainly had not, but I was just passable for general use in chorus singing. Well, I enjoyed that a great deal more than if I had been a solo singer—it was like playing football or any other game, in a team.

A youngster who is exceptionally good at anything, especially if it is a thing where he has not had to work hard for it, is very apt to become swollen-headed. This is particularly the case with singers. The only cure for swollen-head is a stern and strong application at the other end. But where a fellow does chorus work he enjoys putting his voice into it not for his own glorification and applause but for the honour of the team. This means every boy singing his best but modulating his voice to be in proper harmony and proportion to the rest— in other words playing in his place and playing the game not for himself but for his side.

But even choirs can become too cocky about themselves if people make too much of them.

I would therefore always impress upon singers this point: Remember that you didn't make your voice and therefore you needn't be conceited about it and sing merely to win applause. The Creator has lent you that voice and remember that through it you may be touching some man or woman's heart unknown to yourself. In this way you may be passing to them a message from God.

So when you sing, sing with your heart and with reverence.

'Scouting' and woodcraft were, above all others, the things which appealed to B-P in his early days at school. He acknowledged this in an article *The School of the Copse* which he wrote for *The Greyfriar* on the fiftieth anniversary of the school's removal to Godalming:

It was only the other day—it can't be fifty years ago—that I was learning to snare rabbits in the Copse of the new Charterhouse, and to cook them, for secrecy, over the diminutive fire of a bushman. I learned too how to use an axe, how to walk across a gully on a felled tree trunk, how to move silently through the bush so that one became a comrade rather than an interloper among the birds and animals that lived there. I knew how to hide my tracks, how to climb a tree and 'freeze' up there while authorities passed below, forgetting that they were anthropoi, beings capable of looking up (or was it perhaps that they were real men who refrained from looking up, knowing that they would discover one?). And the birds, the stoats, the water-voles that I watched and knew.

Was it fifty years ago that I formed one of the joyous company detailed to bring the canoes from Oxford to Godalming? Fifty years since Sergeant-Major George Ford taught us the marksmanship that was later on to help one to one's share of big game far afield?

These things stand out as if they were of yesterday. Cricket. Football. Athletics. Yes, I enjoyed them too; but they died long ago, they are only a memory like much that I learned at school. It was in the Copse that I gained most of what helped me in after life to find the joy of living.

There have been many discussions and many statements as to how, when and where *Scouting for Boys* originated. Sometimes the scene has been laid in Mafeking, sometimes in the Army in peacetime, sometimes at a certain camp on Brownsea Island.

But I would look further back than all of these. I would look back over a century and peep into that copse at the 'new' Charterhouse and see the young 'Bathing-Towel' intent upon his fire-making.

3 India

Take up the white man's burden,
Have done with childish days.

Rudyard Kipling

When B-P said goodbye to Charterhouse it was with the idea of going up to Oxford. His brother George had distinguished himself at Balliol, and it was some disappointment to him to be pronounced, after a brief examination by the then Master of Balliol, the great Dr Jowett, as 'not quite up to Balliol form'. But, in any case, something intervened which was destined to change the whole course of his career.

Seeing the advertisement of an open examination for direct commissions to the Army he determined to try his luck at it, not, as he said, with any very great hopes of passing in his first attempt. Greatly to his own surprise and that of his friends he passed out second for cavalry and fourth for infantry out of over seven hundred candidates. Or, as Dr Haig-Brown admitted—'By his school instruction, *and much more by the help of his mother wit*, he took a distinguished place in the competition!'

The successful candidates were drafted to Sandhurst for a two years' course of instruction, but the first six in the list were excused this preliminary training. So it came about that, though he only left school in June, B-P received his commission in September of the same year, thereby gaining two years' start over his contemporaries.

It was a sudden change from the sheltered life of a public school to a crack cavalry regiment.

Hitherto his education had cost his family next to nothing and though he was entering an expensive profession, his one idea now was to continue to put them to as little cost as possible. He determined to live on his pay, a thing generally considered impossible in the cavalry; but pay was better in India than in England, though the preliminary expenses of outfit were rather more. So it was fortunate that he was ordered to India at the age of nineteen.

The 13th Hussars, to which regiment he had been gazetted sub-lieutenant, was the same which, as the 13th Light Dragoons, had formed the right of the cavalry line in the famous Charge of the Light Brigade at Balaclava. When B-P joined the Regiment it was stationed at Lucknow and was under command of Colonel John Miller, shortly to be succeeded by Colonel Baker Russell, under whom the regiment gained for itself the nickname of 'The Baker's Dozen'.

The SS *Serapis* left Portsmouth via Queenstown for India on 30th October 1876, with the young Hussar as a passenger. He sent to his mother a very full and descriptive diary of his life on board, from which I quote a few extracts:

October 30th. D. and I went round Pandemonium (the name used to describe their sleeping quarters) last night at about twelve, swinging all the fellows in their hammocks to make them sick. . . .

November 2nd. It is rare fun on board—we felt such swells as we dashed ashore yesterday in the steam launch. . . . They talk about getting up some theatricals on board, so I shall apply for a part.

November 3rd. We left Queenstown. All the inhabitants turned out to cheer us off. Even the roofs of the houses were crowded and all the windows full of waving handkerchiefs.

November 4th. We found ourselves in the Bay of Biscay. I had to go on watch from twelve to four p.m. and again from twelve to four a.m. in the night with two other officers and a guard of sixty men. We had to visit the sentries all over the ship every hour.

November 6th. We saw several porpoises and a shark all close under us playing about by the screw. That night we saw a light-house off the Portuguese coast.

November 8th. I was the first to see a Spaniard. At ten-thirty we passed Gibraltar. I took three little pencil sketches but as we went steaming past at full speed they are very unfinished.

November 12th. *I get up at about seven a.m. and slip on a great coat and a pair of slippers and run up to the bathroom and wait till my turn comes to bathe. About a quarter to eight I am dressed and go and do a little Hindustani till eight-thirty. Then I have breakfast, eggs, coffee, toast, coldmeats, mutton chops, fish, etc. At ten-thirty, there is a parade and I go to my Company, composed of men of the 68th Regiment. From eleven to twelve sit on deck listening to the Band. Twelve-thirty. Lunch, bread, cheese, salad and beer. From one to four playing quoits, single stick, boxing, etc. At four dress for dinner at four-thirty. At six change into frock coat again and go and hear the nigger minstrels sing. At eight we have tea, bread and butter and jam. Eight-thirty till ten-thirty go to the deck-house and talk with the ladies, and then to bed.*

November 13th. Malta. *We came in here yesterday. I went ashore with some other fellows and went over the Governor's Palace and saw a review and the monastery of the Capuchins. . . . Malta is a fine place.*

November 17th. *Have you ever heard of the blue waters of the Mediterranean? If you don't believe it just come here and you will see a blue there is no mistaking. A robin and a wagtail were on board, i.e. flying about and settling on the rigging. They had come with us from Malta. Where they get food I don't know. Talking about birds, tell G. to notice this fact in his hand-book, when we started from Portsmouth two sparrows accompanied us to the Land's End where they left us. When we left Queenstown a robin, a lark, and a starling came out with us. The starling soon went back again but the robin and lark came with us until we were out of sight of land but were not to be seen next morning.*

During this afternoon a stage was rigged up on the poop, perfectly made, a little theatre with stage footlights, drop curtain, entrances and passages, all made of canvas and flags. In the evening we had a performance. I spouted the prologue which had been written by the Captain, then came Whitebait at Greenwich, *after which* The Area Belle *in which I played Pitcher. . . . The Captain said he was very pleased and asked to keep the playbill I had painted.*

*November 18th. Arrived Port Said. . . . It was a very odd sight to
see the men coaling the ship by night with great braziers full of
burning coals set up as lamps. There was nothing to do on shore so
we were not sorry to enter the Suez Canal. But it is a dreary
scene, low banks of mud, beyond these on one side a sandy desert,
on the other a lagoon stretching away on the horizon. . . . I wish
you were here, it is such fine weather, not a cloud in the sky and
not too hot. All this morning we have been passing flocks and
flocks and millions of flamingos. The Canal has gradually got much
narrower, in fact there are only about three yards to spare on
either side of the ship, consequently we have been aground two or
three times. At three p.m. we passed Ismalia. . . . After dinner we
went ashore on to the desert in a narrow boat that had followed us
for some way. Some fellows played 'Hi Cockalorum'; others,
myself among them, set fire to some of the bushes that grow in the
sand every few yards; then one of us started off with a great fog-
horn belonging to the ship and led the rest of us a chase all about in
the desert. The fire was our rendezvous. Others went bathing in
the canal. Others fished for mullet of which we had seen several
shoals.*

*November 20th. This morning when I got on deck we were already
under weigh and had passed through the great Salt Lake. We
expect to reach Suez about one p.m. The weather is beautiful but a
little chilly. I have not yet changed from my English underclothing
and still wear a waistcoat under my uniform and am glad to sit in
the sun. After twelve, however, everybody gets under the awning.
From Suez we get right away to Bombay which we expect to reach
on December 6th.*

December 6th. Arrived at Bombay at seven-thirty.

I have quoted the above extracts from his letters home, because
they show something of their nineteen-year-old author's tastes,
hobbies, and talents most of which he retained to the end of his
life. The interest in birds and animals, the skill with pen and
pencil, the love for acting and harmless practical joking, and the
interest in his work, are all shown as well as a real interest in
people, places and things.

B-P's life during those early days in India, where he spent the years from 1876 to 1883, with one interval of leave, was described by himself in his delightful book *Indian Memories* published in 1915, and copiously illustrated by the author both in line and colour.

Both from the letters written from 1876 onwards, and from his book written nearly forty years later, we judge those Indian days to have been very happy ones, full of work and play and sport, of good comradeship and steady progress in soldiering.

At the end of his first month in Lucknow he wrote to his mother:

My day is occupied thus. At seven-thirty my bearer wakes me and my kitmutgar [servant] *brings in chota hazaree, i.e. a plate of buttered toast and a cup of tea. They then make their salaams and retire, after which I have a bathe and wash and as I come running out of the bathroom in my trousers only, the old bearer who is waiting just outside the door of the bedroom, pops my 'hasher'* [vest] *over my head and then proceeds to dress me, which being done I mount my pony and, accompanied by my syce or running groom, I canter off to the riding school, a place enclosed by four mud walls about four feet high, in which we ride from eight to ten. At ten we go back to the Mess where we have the same sort of breakfast as you have, only with my own kitmutgar waiting upon me. Then return to bungalow (about 200 yards from Mess) and get into frock coat and overalls. At eleven-thirty I go off on my pony again to the stables of my troop (B. Troop). Here I walk up and down till a quarter to one seeing that the horses are being properly groomed. At one I go to the bungalow of my troop and walk through to see that the beds, clothing, etc., are clean and tidy. Then I go and sit outside the Orderly room door with the other officers, in case the Colonel should wish to speak to me. At two p.m. I ride back to Mess and have lunch, or tiffin as we call it, after which I go back to my bungalow and put on stable jacket and sword, and at three ride off to the barracks where I have sword and carbine drill till four-thirty. At four-thirty come back to my bungalow, change for dinner which is at seven-thirty. At ten return to my downy couch.*

The young soldier soon adapted himself to his new life and his letters home during the next two years abound with boyish descriptions of his work and play, of his successes and accidents,

B

---

of riding-horses bought and sold (each one apparently more superb than the last), of parties at Government House where his success as a singer and actor made him a welcome guest, of his progress in the riding school and on parade, of his companions, his clothes, his surroundings and his expenses (his monthly accounts were regularly sent home for inspection); and where words failed (e.g. in describing some wonderful fancy dress or remarkable piece of scenery) he would resort to his pencil.

The burden of many a boy's letters home under similar circumstances would have been 'Send me more money'. With B-P it was rather 'Send me more comic songs'. His appetite for play-books and songs was insatiable, and his family must have had a difficult task to keep him always supplied. Every letter bears the same refrain: 'What about those songs? I am awfully hard up for them.'

Reading between the lines of some of his letters we realise what a struggle it must have been for him to live as simply as he did and yet to retain his popularity with so many better-off comrades. Not every newly joined subaltern would dare to make himself unusual in the ways B-P adopted. But he was popular from the beginning and so could afford to be independent.

'I don't know whether I told you,' he wrote a month or two after joining, 'that I have altogether given up smoking. . . . It saves a big item in the mess bill.'

And again:

At dinner I drink very little, a bottle of soda with a glass of sherry in it. Most people take great silver cups of claret, etc., but I feel much healthier after a little drink, although I am thirsty enough to drink a dozen cups full—and you can imagine the expense comes somewhat different in the end. I am keeping my mess bills very low by drinking very little and taking no extras in the way of fruit, etc. Then, by staying in the mess during the day I don't have to employ punkah coolies,* etc., in my bungalow, which is a saving of about twenty rupees a month.'

To the actual work of commanding men he took like a duck to

* *Punkahs are or were large palm-leaf fans; coolies were hired native labourers.*

water, as this small anecdote of his first inspection shows. It was the rule at this time (almost a hundred years ago of course) that every man should wear round his waist a thick piece of flannel known as a cholera-belt, and many and various were the efforts to evade wearing this hot, prickly and understandably unpopular addition to one's clothes. At such inspections the soldiers were drawn up in two ranks, and having inspected the rear rank, and having seen every man open his shirt and display his cholera-belt, B-P moved to the front rank. As he did so he saw (out of an 'eye at the back of his head') one of the men step from the front rank to the already inspected rear rank—and it happened to be the only one whose name he knew. But B-P completed his front-rank inspection before saying coolly and pleasantly: 'Now, Hardcastle, we should all like to see the colour of *your* belt. Stand out!' The discomforted Hardcastle stepped forward and revealed the fact that he had no belt and, amidst the laughter of his comrades, was awarded the punishment of wearing two belts until further notice.

Towards the end of his second year in India, the climate, the hard work necessary for the forthcoming garrison examination, the many demands of his social life, his rather Spartan way of living all began to take their toll. But when, despite a bout of fever, he took his examination in June, 1878, he passed First Class with a 'special credit' for surveying, the only one given in India that year; and in consequence his lieutenant's commission was ante-dated two years. But his health was not what it ought to be, and, on the doctor's advice he applied for a medical board, which passed him as really quite ill and needing leave to England.

4 India Again

*'One crowded hour of glorious life
is worth an age without a name.'*

Thomas Osbert Mordaunt

Eighteen months in England (during which time he went through the Musketry course at Hythe and passed First Class with extra certificate) completely restored Robert Baden-Powell to health and at the end of 1880 he was delighted to be able to set out in the *Serapis* to rejoin his regiment in India. He had recovered his high spirits:

October 3rd. Woke at five this morning and played the ocarina to Shreiber's banjo and Burns' penny whistle (the other blokes in my cabin) until we had aroused everybody. . . . I'd give anything to have twenty of those buzzing instruments on board, my only one has created a most pleasing sensation.

Now these were the famous Indian Northwest Frontier days (which you can read about for example in Rudyard Kipling's wonderful book *Kim* and which incidentally will show you vividly the kind of place India was when B-P was a serving soldier there). Just over the border was Afghanistan and as Britain was very suspicious of Russia's intentions there and believed that Russia had designs in India, she also believed it essential to keep Afghanistan free from Russian influence and indeed under her own. There was much unrest and intrigue, and in 1880, a number of Afghan chiefs who disliked British interference in their country's affairs, assembled their warriors, proclaimed a jahad or holy war against the British and on 27th July completely routed a British army which was admittedly numerically inferior.

Lieutenant-General Sir Frederick Roberts, VC, who was in Kabul, quickly assembled a large military force and by a remarkable and famous march of 313 miles in twenty days over mountain ranges and stretches of desert reached Kandahar and defeated the Afghans. It was to Kandahar that B-P's regiment under Sir Baker Russell had been ordered, and where B-P soon joined them. On 2nd January, 1881, B-P reported:

I went to Maiwand with the reconnoitring squadron last week. Colonel St. John, General Nicholson, and several other swells went with us; it was a very jolly three days' outing and I wouldn't have missed it for anything. The battlefield was very much as it was left, any amount of dead horses, lines of cartridge cases, wheel tracks and hoof marks quite clear, dead men in heaps (most had been hurriedly buried and dug up again by dogs), clothes and accoutrements all over the place. I brought back a shell, the hoof of an EB (RHA) horse, a bloody bit of belt and a leaf out of Sir G. Wolseley's pocket-book. I have since had to make two maps of the field for General Wilkinson and the C-in-C and the Colonel has asked me to do one for him to send to Sir Garnet Wolseley.

The maps in question probably had a good deal to do, indirectly, with the ultimate success of B-P's soldiering career, as they were sent round to many leading authorities for use at the court-martial on the officers concerned in the defeat at Maiwand.

One amusing incident in connection with these maps occurs in a letter home, dated 3rd April, concerning some theatricals:

Last night I had to wear a bonnet in one piece, so I had an old map of the Maiwand battle I did some time back and sent this over to the tailor to use as stiffening for the bonnet. Later he told me that there were eleven sergeants and people wanting the loan of the bonnet when I had done with it. Why do you think? To copy out the map of the battle to send home to their pals.

The days were happy ones and filled with incident. As B-P wrote:

There was indeed no lack of occupation. One day we would be hunting up one of the bands of robbers in an adjacent pass, only to find that 'the brutes had gone', as I phrased it, so I made a map of the pass for Sir Baker instead. Another day I would be sent out reconnoitring with a troop; or enjoying a picnic as if war were a thing unheard of; a third would find me in charge of an inlying picket which meant sitting all ready in my tent with my horse saddled the whole day and my troop the same, ready to turn out and to march within two minutes of the alarm. Then at dusk we would go out of camp about a mile, post vedettes (mounted sentries) and send out patrols every hour throughout the night to examine the neighbourhood. We would take two tents with us, but keep dressed with our horses saddled all ready to turn out. At daybreak we would move out to examine a post some five miles off and then back to camp. Sometimes it was so cold at night that instead of putting up the tent our men would prefer to roll themselves up in it on the ground. They had to wear Balaclava caps, that is knitted nightcaps which came down all over the head and neck, with eye-holes to look out from. We succeeded in getting a great deal of experience, as we were constantly expecting attacks and the long bitterly cold nights on outpost duty hardened us thoroughly.

Shortly after their arrival, a regimental concert was given, during which there was a stir at the back of the hall where the men were sitting. In walked a General and proceeded up the centre aisle, telling the men loudly to sit down at which, seeing their important visitor, they naturally stood up.

Colonel Baker Russell, who was seated in the front row, on hearing the commotion, rose and came forward to meet his unexpected guest, and led him to a seat.

But the bluff old fellow showed himself ready to join in the fun and suggested, somewhat to the Colonel's surprise, that he was prepared to go on the stage and give them a song. This offer was greeted with loud applause and it was not until the visitor was half way through the Major-General's song from *The Pirates of Penzance* that the Colonel realised that he had been 'had' and that his friend was no other than his young subaltern B-P who, knowing that his Colonel had not yet met a certain General in Kandahar, had borrowed the General's uniform from a friendly ADC.

The Colonel took the joke in good part and never forgot it.

It was at Kandahar that Baden-Powell carried out a piece of tracking which won him the praise of his Commanding Officer and probably had a good deal to do with his early promotion. One night, there was a terrific hurricane and hailstorm, the horses took fright and broke loose, rushing about with their picketing ropes and tent pegs attached, and it took some hours to get them all collected and calmed down again. All were eventually recaptured except one, the horse ridden by the Regimental Sergeant-Major and therefore one of the best in the regiment. B-P determined that this horse should be found and he set out alone on his charger 'Dick' to look for the hoof tracks. After some searching he came upon the trail of a horse galloping away from camp. Following up the trail for two or three miles he found it led up into the mountains over such steep ground that he would have to follow it on foot. Fortunately Dick had been trained by his master to stand still for no matter how long, so he could safely be left below. Up the mountain B-P climbed, following the trail until at last he was rewarded by the sight of a horse's outline against the sky, right away at the top of the mountain and there, after a long climb, he found the missing beast shivering with cold and badly cut about by the iron picketing-peg which was still hanging on to him. Great was the joy in camp when the triumphant procession returned, and from that day Baden-Powell was a marked man.

The regiment's next move was to Quetta and it was during this march that B-P had the misfortune to shoot himself in the leg with his revolver while on a night raid at the Kojak Pass, and had to make the rest of the journey in a 'dhoolie' or covered stretcher.

On arrival at Quetta he had to lie up for some weeks and to endure considerable pain and discomfort while the doctors 'did a bit of gardening' as he expressed it, on his foot in order to locate and extract the bullet.

He spent these days drawing, having Hindustani lessons, studying French and Persian for possible future use, and planning concerts and theatrical entertainments for the next few months. He kept an eagle eye on home productions in this direction. 'Look out for the first production of Gilbert and Sullivan's new opera and post it off to me with sketches of dresses, etc.' was the command given in a letter home which foreshadowed the production shortly afterwards of one of the regiment's most successful efforts.

Quetta was an unhealthy spot and there was a good deal of sickness among the officers and men. B-P found that a great preventive of illness was to give them plenty of occupation and amusement in their spare time and to this end he and his brother officers were continually organising gymkhanas, concerts and theatricals.

He was now musketry instructor to the Regiment, which brought in a good deal of extra work, and what was of importance to him, a little extra pay.

After Quetta came a six weeks' march of 900 miles to Muttra, on the River Jumna. Here with his brother officers he became passionately interested in two Indian sports—polo and what was called 'pig-sticking' but was actually wild boar hunting.

It must be remembered that in those days, nearly a hundred years ago, the cavalry were an essential branch of the army and cavalry-men had to be expert horsemen. But these sports helped to provide the necessary training for those who could afford them. Wild boars are amongst the most savage of jungle animals—the real Kings of the Jungle, it is said—and hunting them on horseback with spears needed immense courage and skill.

B-P, who had courage and horse-riding skill in plenty, took up pig-sticking with such enthusiasm and success that later, in 1884, he wrote the authoritative book on the subject and won the most coveted honour in this sport, the Kadir Cup. This event he described in a letter home:

Yes, I won the Kadir Cup, a thing beyond all my hopes, in fact I can hardly believe it now. There were fifty-four horses running for it. The whole fifty-four were divided by lot into parties of four, then each of these parties had an umpire to look after it. He took his party about in the jungle and when he saw a pig he told the four to ride it; away they all go and the man who first spears it wins the heat. Well, there were fourteen parties in the first round of heats and I was in three different ones, having three horses, all of which I won. Then all the winners of the first round were divided into four parties again, in three of which I had a horse running. Well, the four winners of this round were to contest for this Cup. Squeers was the first horse of mine I rode in this round. I was first at the pig, stuck at home and just missed him, the spear caught in some grass and was twisted out of my hand—and the next chap came up and stuck the pig. So I lost that heat, but I won both my others with Patience and Hagarene. So of the four horses competing for the Cup I owned two. Well, I couldn't ride two at once so Macdougall rode Patience and I rode Hagarene. Such excitement. Twenty elephants with on-lookers, fellows up in trees, others riding with us to see the fun. Away goes a great pig. 'Ride'—and away we go. Hagarene soon gets away from the rest. The pig dashes into thick jungle but I'm pretty close to him and can just see him every now and then. Great tussocks of grass, six feet high, Haggy bounding through them, then twenty yards of open ground, then into a fresh patch of jungle thicker than the other. Suddenly bang, down we go—no we don't—very nearly though. One of the grass tussocks had a solid pillar of hard earth concealed in it which the mare struck with her chest. Now then, we're close on him—get the spear ready—now ready to reach him, suddenly a bright green sort of hedge appears in front as the pig disappears through it. Haggy leaps it and there, eight feet below it, is a placid pond, the pig goes plump under water and Haggy and self ditto almost on top of him. Right down we go to any depth—a deal of struggling—striking out—hanging on to weeds, etc. and I emerge on the far bank and see Haggy climbing out too, and away she goes for camp, and the pig I can just see skulking away in some reeds. Up come the other three men in the heat and look over the hedge at me. I point out the pig and away they go, and Macdougall gets first to him and spears him and so wins the Cup for me, and a funny object I look when all the fellows come up to congratulate me, covered with mud and water and garlanded with weeds.

Meanwhile his Army Career was progressing: in 1883 he was appointed adjutant of the 13th Hussars and was promoted Captain.

When the Duke of Connaught went out to India in 1884 as GOC Meerut, Baden-Powell was temporarily attached to his staff. In the same year he was employed as brigade-major to the Cavalry at manoeuvres.

B-P's activities in the pig-sticking field not unnaturally caused his family at home no small anxiety, and many were the warnings which he received. 'I will certainly give up pig-sticking in two months' time,' he wrote in reply to one letter, 'that will be when the pig-sticking season is over.'

Next to pig-sticking in his estimation came polo, at which game he frequently represented the 13th:

Polo I play three times a week regularly and love it more and more. That's the great drawback in England, that we can't get polo nearly so good or anything like so inexpensive as it is out here, and if it weren't for polo I am positively certain I couldn't have stuck out three hot weathers without leave.

In addition to his office work which, as adjutant, he now had to add to his other duties, B-P found opportunity for a good deal of writing and sketching on his own account, and the cheques in payment for articles and sketches came in very usefully to swell his banking account.

In 1884 he published a book on *Reconnaissance and Scouting*, and exhibited sketches at the Simla Exhibition which were 'highly commended'.

He made occasional journeys to Simla and other hill stations and was a lively addition to the balls, theatricals, and other amusements there. But he was never so happy as when at work, and the camp life with its pig-sticking and shooting had far more to commend itself to him than the tennis and picnics of the hills.

Then, at the end of 1884 the 13th Hussars were ordered to Natal to act if necessary in conjunction with Sir Charles Warren's expedition to Bechuanaland.

So, after much packing up, selling of horses and property, amassing of new outfits, etc. B-P said farewell to the delights of India and entered with enthusiasm upon his new surroundings at the Cape, 'the very thing I had been hoping for'.

General Sir Charles Callwell, in his *Reminiscences* refers to his first meeting with B-P as follows:

I was detained at Deolalee for three or four days, during which time the 13th Hussars turned up on their way from India to South Africa. Baden-Powell, whose name I had often heard, was the adjutant, and on the night that they spent at the place he happened to sit opposite to me at dinner. He was in his absurdest mood, playing all manner of monkey tricks, imitating the various performers in an orchestra, and so forth, and he had the man sitting next to me and myself in such fits of laughing that when the meal came to an end we discovered to our concern that we had had practically nothing to eat. We had to sneak back after the room was cleared, and order poached eggs to keep body and soul together till the morning.

5 The Cape

Let us prove the silent places, let us see what luck betide us . . .
The wild is calling, calling—let us go.

Robert Service

'Eight of us are going to start off to ride a hundred miles tomorrow and see how fast we can do it,' wrote Baden-Powell when he had been a few weeks in Natal, and on 7th March 1885 the *Morning Post*, a national newspaper of those days, published the following paragraph:

Last year we were told a good deal too much about the rides of certain Austrian cavalry officers, considering that England can always compete with continental feats of riding. As an instance of what our own cavalrymen will do for mere pleasure it may be noted that on the 27th January, Captain Baden-Powell, adjutant of the 13th Hussars, and six other officers of the 13th, rode from Durban to Pietermaritzburg (fifty-six miles) in four hours and twenty-one minutes. After resting their horses for a couple of hours the officers remounted and rode to Pinetown in four hours and ten minutes, arriving in first-rate condition and only eager to start off on fresh horses for another hundred miles.

The time in Natal, on the fringe of war but yet not actively engaged in it, was very irksome to one who was longing to see active service. Yet B-P managed to find compensations and was certainly never at a loss for employment. Unaided he carried out a secret reconnaissance of the Natal frontier of 600 miles, which involved some fairly strenuous work both at the time and afterwards

44

in compiling maps and reports. This solitary tour was carried out with the aid of two horses, of which he rode one and led the other alternately. He grew a beard and figured as a newspaper correspondent, or sometimes as an artist or a fisherman.

In July 1885, B-P's elder brother George came out to South Africa as a political adviser. He was an authority on the colonies generally, having visited most of them on official missions, and was subsequently (as Sir George Baden-Powell, KCMG) for fifteen years MP for the Kirkdale Division of Liverpool. He was ten years older than the B-P of this story, and was of the greatest help to him throughout his early career, both through his personal friendship with many influential men of the day and also through his knowledge of the world and experiences of travel, all of which were laid at the feet of his promising young brother. He also undertook the 'fathering' of many of B-P's early books through the press, when their author was too busy and too far away to correct and revise proofs.

In July 1885, B-P obtained two months' leave, and set off with a party of friends, six in all, including the celebrated South African hunter, Reuben Beningfield, for a big game shooting trip near Inhambane, an old slave port in Portuguese East Africa. In his diary of the Expedition B-P wrote:

14th July. Learned that a force was out from Inhambane keeping natives quiet in our shooting district. Military force consists of one officer, twenty-four white men, two guns, artillery, infantry. The officers are Portuguese, the men mainly natives, chiefly convicts, as the Army here is a kind of reformatory. Native levies are called out from time to time and armed with 'Brown Bess' and flint locks, no ammunition. Inhambane is a small town under Portuguese government, 300 years old. Consists of custom house, barracks, Governor's house, town office, ruined church, houses of shipping agents; native part of town a well-kept arrangement of native huts in palm groves.

20th. Saw native way of making a cigarette by licking a dried plantain leaf and rolling tobacco in it. Our party consists of six English, ninety-five carriers, seven servants, two hunters, two cooks, and thirty escort—total 142.

21st. Heard that the tribe here were out on the war-path against

*the next tribe and that we were supposed to be coming to join in the
row.*

*22nd. Breakfasted in the kraal in the 'enemy's country'. Chief
civil and told us where to go to get game. Bee-hives used in this country
are a cylinder of bark about four feet long and eighteen inches in
diameter, covered at both ends and a few holes bored in the sides.
These are put up in the branches of the bare white trees near each
village.*

*23rd. The correct way to wash your hands in this village (owing to
the scarcity of water) is to fill your mouth with water and then let a
thin stream trickle on to your hands while you wash.*

*25th. Saw a good deal of lion and hippo spoor. At breakfast a
messenger from the King of the country to say that his ambassadors
were coming to see us. Shortly after four of them appeared and had a
talk. They said the Portuguese were raiding in their country on one
side and the Zulu and other tribes threatening them on the other, and
that there was every chance of their being wiped out between the two—
wanted therefore to place themselves under English protection. We
told them we had no power to receive them as allies but would represent
their case to the Portuguese Governor. In the meantime might we
shoot in their country? This appeared to satisfy them and they said
we could go and shoot wherever we pleased.*

*The gut of a buck or sheep threaded on a stick and roasted over the
fire is an excellent morsel—like sausage skin lined with marrow.*

27th. I shot a hippo.

*28th. Shot a red buck. Hit a hippo on the nose. Shot a goose with
rifle. Hippo's tongue a good dish like ox tongue.*

*29th. Saw a herd of water-buck trekking from water to woods—
followed and stalked for two miles but did not get within shot.*

*3rd August. After dinner the girls and children of the village, down
to those who had only just gained the use of their legs, came and sang
and danced; some of them dancing rather well. One figure consisting
of one dancer selecting another and both squatting down in the centre of
the ring, while one went through the motions of shaving the other's
head.*

*5th. Ambassadors from another chief came asking us to take him
under English rule and to decide a case of cattle ownership. It took
about an hour's palaver to tell them to go to blazes. While riding*

along noticed a number of stumps and ant hills. Drew attention to the fact that they might easily be mistaken for big game, when they suddenly resolved themselves into a herd of water-buck. I nearly had an altercation with a big yellow snake while stalking. Saw a buck, loosed Captain and rode him, a grand gallop, till he went to bay in a waterhole, where I put a bullet through his head.

6th. Disturbed in the night by lions who caused three bullocks, sent by the King, to stampede. One of them bellowed shortly after in a distressed kind of way. Sent out to follow bullocks and in a short time a mournful procession returned carrying the hide, hoofs, shank bones and skull, all that was left of one bullock. The men had come on the lions taking their last licks, about half a mile from camp—four of them, two of them males. Went out after the lions, all the trackers taking shields and assegais. At the scene of the kill not a scrap of meat was left; then proceeded to follow the spoor through the bush, mostly on foot, for five hours and finally found ourselves on the track of one big lion. We sighted him going across a piece of open and galloped after him but he got into the dense bush ahead of us. Here we followed him on foot with great difficulty; finding a continuation of this bush leading on to open ground we made the trackers beat the bush, tapping their shields with their assegais, while we posted ourselves in the open to catch him as he came out, but he failed to do so and we never saw him or his spoor again.

16th. On the march, when I started to overtake the rest after stalking wildebeeste, I found my way back to their trail by sun and landmarks and then followed it up easily, all diverging tracks having been marked with a few strokes in the sand to show that they were not to be followed (tip for advanced Scouts).

23rd. Begin to fear that I shall be taken for an escaped convict when I get home. I go dodging and slinking along always on the look out for spoor or game.

24th. A party of native hunters with guns were in camp during the day, having got wind of meat there, which showed how shot over the country is. Their way of shooting is to lie out day and night for days on some favourite feeding ground of game till they get a close shot.

26th. Our regular food at this period is breakfast of porridge, standing stew (rice, and meat of any game or birds we killed, always kept handy, ready to serve up) and tea; dinner, stew, fry, 'bachem' (toddy)—the juice of palm plants (water is unobtainable) and dampers. These we make very light by using bachem in making the dough instead of water and putting in lots of baking-powder—let stand for an hour and then fry or, better, bake them by inverting an earthenware pot over a plate of them and standing them on hot wood ashes and lighting a pyramid fire over the pot. If left all night they come out hard and crisp like rusks and can be kept for days. Ate a lot of kaffir oranges on the march, they are hard round fruit which, when broken open give you a coffee-coloured pulp full of big pips, till I got used to it the flavour was that of pomade.

It was at Inhambane that B-P won for himself from the natives the name of M'hlala Panzi 'the man who lies down to shoot' or the man who makes his plans carefully before taking aim. This name followed him throughout his career and, on reading his letters home at that time, one realises how very appropriate it was. He was always making plans—'grouping events' he called it—not only for his own future but for his brothers' careers and his mother's well-being, and for the general comfort and credit of his family. So carefully were his plans laid out and so many irons had he in the fire at the same time that—unlike most youthful dreams—a good many of them became actual accomplished facts.

At the end of 1885 the regiment was ordered home to Norwich and great was their joy to be in England again. 'How I do eat bread and butter and beef and revel in the rain and fog,' wrote B-P to his brother George.

Two years in England—at Norwich, Colchester, and Liverpool—went by very quickly.

In 1886 B-P (with his younger brother Baden, then a subaltern in the Scots Guards) visited Germany and Russia and reported on the Russian manoeuvres to the British War Office. He was also employed as assistant adjutant-general at manoeuvres at Dover, and was on duty as a judge at the Royal Military Tournament.

1887 opened with a visit to the battlefields of the Franco-German war of 1870 when he stayed with a regiment of Uhlans at Strasbourg.

In *My Adventures as a Spy* (re-issued as *The Adventures of a Spy* in 1924) he later wrote down many amusing and instructive accounts of his travels in these various countries, of how he was arrested and escaped, the disguises he used, and so on.

In 1887 he was on duty as a judge at the Royal Military Tournament, and also organised a 'Grand Military Tournament' on his own in Liverpool, in which every man in his squadron of the 13th Hussars took part.

At the end of 1887 he was specially detailed by Lord Wolseley the then Commander-in-Chief of the British Army, who had watched his work at Liverpool, to conduct some cavalry machine-gun trials at Aldershot, and here is that famous soldier's letter to him on that occasion:

Dear Captain Baden-Powell, A recent inspection of the handling of the machine-guns attached to the several regiments of cavalry at Aldershot was anything but a success, attributable apparently to the defective training of the detachments. I am anxious that this defect be remedied and I wish you, as one of the few officers of the Army who have requisite knowledge, to do so. It will be necessary for you to go to Aldershot for about a fortnight, and I want you to let me know when it will be convenient for you to go there. On hearing from you what will be a convenient date for yourself I will communicate officially through your Commanding Officer.

Yours truly, WOLSELEY.

6 Zululand

Een gon yama, gon yama Invooboo
Ya bo, ya bo, Invooboo.

Zulu Chant

At the end of 1887, General Smyth, General Officer Commanding South Africa, who also happened to be B-P's uncle, offered him the post of ADC. This was gladly accepted and in January 1888 he found himself in South Africa once more, the scene of some good soldiering in the past and of triumph for him in the future.

For the first few months after his arrival B-P found that his work as ADC was hardly strenuous enough for his active person. 'I am having a very good time,' he said, 'but feel as if I had been sent here for a complete rest which, at my time of life, seems hardly necessary.' However, there was always the chance of some little war cropping up, so he bided his time, employing himself out of official hours with theatricals, polo, and shooting.

In July of that same year came the longed-for moment when he was able to write:

Here we are, en route for Zululand, the General, Colonel Curtis and I. They say there is to be a fight. The only fear is that it may come off before we get there but we have ordered the steamer to crack on and she is doing so. We leave tomorrow morning for Eshowe en route for the fun.

The cause of the 'fun' was one Dinizulu, the son of the old Chief Cetywayo. After the Zulu war, Lord Wolseley had divided Zululand into eight districts, each under a Chief. Dinizulu was one

50

of these chiefs, and another was John Dunn, a Scottish leader who lived among Zulus from his boyhood and had advised Cetywayo.

Dinizulu raised a rebellion against the British, four tribes joined him, two remained neutral, and two (Dunn's and Usibepu's) joined the British.

As Dinizulu ignored warnings from the British Commissioner, a warrant for his arrest was issued and on 2nd June a party of native police under Major Mansell, supported by 6th Dragoon Guards and mounted infantry, went to Ceza Bush, where Dinizulu was encamped with a following of Usutus, to put the warrant into effect.

They were outnumbered, however, and were obliged to retire. Meantime fresh risings were taking place in all directions. In the east the Usutus surrounded the station of Mr Pretorius, the Assistant Commisioner of the Coast District. He had with him a small force of police and some 300 friendly natives, and with these he was successful in repulsing one attack, but he was soon hemmed in on all sides and news, brought by a runner who had succeeded in getting through the enemy lines, showed him to be in hourly danger.

At this juncture General Smyth with his staff arrived at Eshowe. Without wasting any time the General organised a flying column, composed of 160 Inniskilling Dragoons, a company of Mounted Infantry from the Royal Inniskilling Fusiliers, and about 100 bayonets of the North Staffordshire Regiment, and this column was augmented by a contingent of 2,000 Zulus under John Dunn, and later by 200 mounted Basutus.

The commander of this relief column was Major McKean, of the Inniskilling Dragoons, and with him, as staff officer, went Captain Baden-Powell:

Then followed one of those times of pleasurable excitement known to few but soldiers. The enemy's scouts could be seen on a hill half a mile away, behind which his main body was supposed to be, but in what strength was quite a matter of conjecture. The orders were given for rapidly making a circular laager, or fort, with the baggage waggons, of which the defence was handed over to the Infantry while the Dragoons and Mounted Infantry went off at a trot across the open grassy hills to co-operate with their native allies, who had already sprung from their coil and were eagerly pressing forward at their never tiring jog trot, in that wide, extended, semi-circular formation that constitutes their form of attack. On they went for nearly a mile, the Zulus easily keeping pace with the mounted troops, until at last they topped the high ridge overlooking the enemy's ground. Nothing there! A few forms in the far distance—the last of the enemy's skirmishers— could be descried running their best to gain the cover of a vast tract of reeds and swamp into which it would be perfectly useless to attempt to follow them. In another moment the heliographs are flashing, and soon after the column is once more stringing along the track towards Mr Pretorius's station. At length on the 8th July the relief column had arrived without opposition at its bivouac not more than eight miles from its goal. Soon after night fall a spy was sent forward with orders to communicate if possible with the besieged, and at two in the morning he returned with the welcome news that he had been successful in his attempt, and had brought back a note from the magistrate himself telling of the safety of his little garrison and warning his relievers of the presence of a force of the enemy not far from them. However, nothing was seen of it during the march the next morning and before nine o'clock the garrison turned out with alacrity to welcome the head of the column whose advent they had waited for so long. Although there was no trained military engineer amongst them, necessity, the mother of invention, and commonsense, its father, had led the defenders into building a very strong little fort on a knoll overlooking the Umsindusi Valley. The fort itself was little more than forty yards square consisting of a sod parapet surrounded by a ditch and a strong and high thorn fence. Outside this stood straw huts in which the garrison lived and these were again surrounded by an impassable thorn fence. At the foot of the knoll, some eighty yards from the fort, were the huts occupied by Sokwetchata's people (the friendly tribe) and kraals for the cattle. It appears that there had been a second attack by the enemy on the post on the 10th June, originating in an attack on some of Sokwetchata's men, who were out gathering forage. The garrison made a sally, as on the first occasion, and were on the point of arriving within striking distance when an unaccountable panic seized Sokwetchata's people, and they turned tail and made a bolt for the fort, and naturally the police and whites had to follow suit.

Once under the protection of its cover they were perfectly safe, and the enemy soon drew off, out of range, but in this short action the defence had lost forty men killed and fourteen wounded. Many of these latter were in a bad way as they seemed to have no idea of the simplest treatment of wounds, and consequently the doctor, Surgeon Hackett, found a good deal of work to do on his arrival.

With the promptness that distinguished all the movements of this expedition, plans were drawn out and a site selected for the erection of a new fort—since the original one was commanded at a very short distance by the surrounding hills—and within a few hours of their arrival the troops had made good progress with it, so much so that by the following morning it was deemed safe to leave the infantry detachment to garrison the embryo work while the mounted troops started to return. 'Boots and Saddles' had already sounded and the baggage trains were already being inspanned, when the look-out sentries reported scouts of the enemy on the neighbouring hills. The march was therefore countermanded and John Dunn's Zulus were directed to make a reconnaissance with a view to finding the enemy if he were anywhere within reasonable distance, which was doubtful as the look-out men had reported a large force visible in the far distance making all speed away from the neighbourhood. In an incredibly short space of time heavy smoke began to ascend from distant kraals, without any accompaniment of musketry, which to those watching was a sign that the enemy had abandoned his villages to the tender mercies of the relieving force, and fled. While the reconnaissance was being carried out the troops left in camp were busily employed building the new fort into shape.

Fort McKean, as it was christened after the commander of the expedition, might be deemed impregnable in this country, and yet it had but little of the Vauban or any other 'system' about it; an engineer would look upon it with horror as a violation of all the principles of defence, but it was designed by two cavalry officers (McKean and Baden-Powell) who, guided by commonsense and past experiences, have made a work capable of withstanding any attack by Zulus with least possible expenditure of men.

B-P noted in his diary for 11th July that 'the parade of Dunn's impi was a very fine sight, they formed in a huge semi-circle round the Chief, all singing a solemn kind of chant in parts.' This chant was the one once known to thousands of Scouts as the 'Eengonyama Chorus' and that was where B-P first heard it.

On the return march the column was divided into three bodies and went by three different routes in order to break up any large bodies of the enemy.

The doctor having been left behind with the garrison at Fort McKean, it fell to B-P to act as doctor to the sick and wounded with his column, and for such a task he had prepared himself some years earlier by studying 'First Aid'.

It was on this return journey that, after a slight skirmish, one of the Zulus was seen carrying a wounded girl on his back. It was so unusual for a Zulu to spare, much less to save, an enemy that investigations were made and it turned out that the wounded girl was his niece. She had been shot through the abdomen. Major McKean and B-P made a fire for her and gave her a restorative. The 'doctor' bandaged her up and got a sack and blanket for her. She had nothing on except a bead girdle and necklace and it was pouring with rain. Uncle Zulu was put in charge of her for the night. In the middle of the night groans were heard and, getting out of his blankets under a waggon, B-P found to his indignation that uncle had wrapped himself up in the sack and left his niece uncovered. On being rebuked he bolted away into the darkness, taking the sack with him. In spite of being wrapped in the officers' waterproof cloaks the girl died. She was buried at daybreak and B-P kept her necklace of black and white beads.

The success of this relief expedition naturally brought great credit both on Major McKean and his staff officer.

B-P's next job was to form an Intelligence Department at the General's headquarters, while Major McKean commanded a second flying column, which was successful in subduing other rebel impis.

It now only remained to capture Dinizulu himself. To this end the General moved his headquarters on 1st August to within twenty miles of the Ceza Bush. From here he threw out lines of posts connecting one with the other so as to hem in completely the Ceza Bush where Dinizulu was encamped. It fell to B-P's lot to make a reconnaissance of the Ceza stronghold. He started off with a mounted force of Dragoons, mounted infantry and natives.

There was a little preliminary fighting at a place known as Fig Tree Store, which the enemy had attacked. B-P was in command of the fight and very nearly got into trouble. During the night his force was laagered* in camp and all was quiet, when he awoke suddenly, smelling something suspicious. He roused his men quietly (they all slept at their posts) and it became apparent that the enemy were creeping up to attack. A few rounds showed them that the British were ready to receive them and they withdrew.

Directly it was light B-P and his force followed them up. They retreated across the border into the Boers' country and took refuge in some caves in the mountain side just across the border, thinking themselves safe. But their pursuers disregarded the border and followed them up, attacked, and defeated them.

The sequel to this was a telegram from the Governor of the Cape to the General, asking the name of the officer who had *committed murder* in a friendly country. But luck was on the side of B-P for he was able to show that the map issued to him by the Government was an old one which showed the mountain that he had attacked to be within the boundary. So he heard no more about it. But the main point of this story is to show how important to a Scout is the sense of *smell*.

The force then proceeded to Ceza Bush, only to discover that Dinizulu, finding himself cornered, had evacuated his position and crossed the border into the Transvaal, taking with him his 2,000 men with their cattle.

In November of the same year he voluntarily submitted to the British authorities. In the meantime the General and his staff had returned to the Cape.

So ended a rising which might, judging from the previous Zulu campaign, have readily burst once more into the flames of war. Confidence was restored, many rebel ringleaders were captured, and the arch-leader Dinizulu driven out of the country.

For his good work in connection with this rising, B-P was appointed Assistant Military Secretary to the General at the Cape, and gained promotion.

* *A laager was a defensive ring of ox-wagons.*

7 Swaziland, Malta and Home

> *To count the life of battle good,*
> *And dear the land that gave you birth,*
> *And dearer yet the brotherhood*
> *That binds the brave of all the earth*

> Henry Newbolt

Back at the Cape once more, B-P began to devise further schemes for adventure, and a brilliant idea came to him of combining a shooting trip down the Zambesi river with the collecting of information required by the Government about the Portuguese territories there. He wrote home at once for a collapsible boat and other necessary gear, and conducted a trial trip before the great African hunter, Frederick Courtney Selous, who 'considered the boat well suited to the purpose'.

The trip never came off, however, as at that juncture General Smyth became Acting Governor and was unable to spare his useful Military Secretary for any length of time. It was a bitter disappointment but B-P 'smiled and whistled' and went cheerily off instead for a few days' shooting.

During this trip he had his first encounter with an elephant, and this is how he described it in his diary for Friday, 12th April, 1889:

After three cups of coffee we started for the forest at six a.m. Cool morning after the rain and lucky it was cool for the walking was simply awful. It has been bad each day but this day we started to go

56

straight through the bush to Couna, sending our horses by the path
with Jourmet junior. The forest was all a dense undergrowth of tree
ferns, bushes, and creepers, etc. the ground all broken up with elephant
spoor and bog holes—scenery like the pictures of tropical jungle but
the reality is not so charming as the picture. The woodcutter told us of
one spot where the elephants certainly were but where it would, to say
the least of it, not be politic to follow them. We had not been going an
hour before we found ourselves in the stronghold of the enemy. And
it was a place; a thick jungle of tree ferns over one's head, entangled
with a dense growth of creeping ferns, and a regular maze of narrow
well-worn holey elephant passages circulating about in it. We got
well into it but found no elephants there; what we should have done
had they been there I don't quite know, but I imagine it would have
depended chiefly on the good feeling of the elephants themselves.

We were rather glad when we got out of this place. Then we
struggled on; breakfast at eight punctually but frugally, viz., one
and a half hard boiled eggs and a cup of milk and one of champagne
(at least many people would have supposed it to have been fresh
spring water but we hypnotised ourselves to believe otherwise).

At ten o'clock after a weary struggle we reached a small open hill.
As we were crossing this Charley (the boy) suddenly said he saw
elephants. We looked and looked with naked eyes and with glasses and
at last after a long time we saw them clearly enough feeding along
some rather open bush on the opposite side of a valley. We got reins
on to all the dogs and started to approach the 'oilyphants' as Jourmet
calls them. Left the dogs and Charley in a safe tree stump, and then
we proceeded to struggle through awfully thick fern jungle up towards
where we had seen the beasts. At last we could hear them in front,
tearing down twigs and giving an occasional snort or a rumbling growl.
We climbed on to tree stumps to get a view over the ferns, and
presently the crashing of branches and cracking of rotten sticks
came nearer till it seemed about fifty yards off—but the jungle was
still too thick for us to see them. Suddenly I saw a branch dragged
down, and there was a great trunk round it and a couple of long
white tusks—and for a second I saw the whole head of an elephant;
enormous it seemed. Two others were then visible to me close by—
i.e. within a hundred yards but too far off to shoot at—directly they
stood still they became as it were invisible; it was only when they

57

moved that they were distinguishable from the forest round about. Presently there was a pause in their crashing and Jourmet excitedly whispered that they had bolted—and so it was although they had made off without a sound. We followed the spoor for some way but it led into heart-breaking ground, and at last sick, tired, and wet through (for we had two heavy cold showers) we gave it up and returned to Charley and the dogs.

During the following summer B-P was sent home to England for short leave and change of air, and while there met Sir Francis de Winton, who was about to start on a mission to Swaziland, then an independent native territory under Umbadine, the King.

The good grazing and the mineral wealth of Swaziland had drawn large numbers of Boers and diggers into the county and the Regent and the young King found themselves in difficulties with the demands made on them for land. The white population numbered a thousand during part of the year. The country was in an unsettled state, and after preliminary investigations it was decided to send a joint British and Boer Commission, under special Commissioners from England and the South African Republic, to make full enquiry and to report on the situation. Sir Francis de Winton was appointed British Commissioner, and on his way via the Cape he picked up B-P and was allowed to add him to his staff as private secretary.

The journey into Swaziland was enlivened with hunting, shooting and fishing.

As usual during his expedition B-P kept a diary: here is his description of Johannesburg, as it was at that time:

Johannesburg itself is a wonderfully big city (30,000 inhabitants), and has only been invented within the last three years. All the bigger buildings and offices are brick or stone with zinc roof. The Grand National Hotel is the best Hotel I have seen so far in S. Africa, accommodates 120 or more, is always full, and charges twenty-five shillings a day. Everything in the way of food or drink is very expensive, especially as they are only just getting in supplies after recent famine, e.g. eggs sixpence each, cabbages four shillings, bottle of milk one shilling., etc. In spite of its richness and good

buildings the town is still unpaved and unlighted at night. *The
streets are therefore always ankle deep either in dust or mud. Mud had
it while we were there.*

While at Johannesburg the party explored a gold mine, the largest
in Johannesburg, which gets 'an average of 8000 oz. per mensem
of gold,' and here is a tip for Scouts from that day's diary:

*We all had candles while below, and I got the knack of carrying them
in a draught—i.e. holding the candle between the second and third
finger with the flame fairly close down to the hand.*

On 29th December B-P wrote to his mother:

*Here we are back in Natal after an unprecedently short journey from
Swaziland. We had good mules and fine weather and we came along
at a tremendous pace, doing in thirteen days what would usually
take about twenty or more, and in wet weather would take probably
from six weeks to two or three months. We are all in excellent health
and I am only sorry it is all over so soon.*

During his absence in Swaziland B-P's future had been under-
going consideration at the Cape. Sir Henry Smyth was offered,
and accepted, the office of Governor and Commander-in-Chief
at Malta, and gave his ADC the opportunity of going with him as
Military Secretary and ADC, with the stipulation, however, that
he must not expect leave to go to any end of the earth where a fight
might be going on. This offer was at once accepted and early in
1890, after a short leave to England, the new Governor and B-P
took up their appointments.

On 1st March Malta was reached and B-P settled down to his
new life of office work, dinners and levées, theatricals and polo.

He had not been there long when Sir Francis de Winton offered
to take him again on his staff on his mission to Uganda. To this
suggestion the Governor of Malta replied shortly: 'I have not the
slightest idea of lending him to Sir F. de Winton or anybody else.'

B-P wrote to his mother:

This is awful, I thought that once Sir F. de Winton had gone I should

*be rid of the longing to be with him, but I feel more and more anxious
to be there. I can't think of anything else. But you can't picture that,
what I should call camp sickness that gets hold of one—a sort of
hunger to be out in the wilds and away from all this easygoing
mixture of office and drawing-room—clerk and butler.*

In spite of these hankerings after active service B-P managed to
enjoy life in Malta to the full. One of his first tasks was to get the
armoury in the Palace properly arranged.

In July the Governor moved his quarters from San Antonio
Palace to Verdala. B-P described his new home as being:

*a very solid old square building—300 years old—with a square tower
at each corner and surrounded by a dry moat. Huge thick walls and
stone floors, frescoed ceilings, dungeons and secret passages all over
the place; one dungeon opens by a tiny passage into my bedroom
and has the staples in the walls to which they tied prisoners and then
burnt them (the walls and ceilings are still smoke-begrimed).*

B-P particularly made a name for himself in Malta as being the
friend and helper of the soldiers and sailors in the garrison and
fleet. Lady Smyth wrote:

*One of the great successes was getting each of the five regiments
stationed in the island to give concerts, one regiment taking charge
of it each month, which caused much competition among the men,
giving them great interest and evening employment in practising and
preparing their respective programmes.*

But perhaps his greatest achievement was the formation of the
Soldiers' and Sailors' Recreation Club. For two years before it was
possible to open it B-P was getting up concerts and entertainments
to raise the necessary funds for the project, and on 31st March
1893 he wrote proudly from the:

SOLDIERS' AND SAILORS' CLUB, MALTA:
*What do you think of the above heading? Well, it means I have got
my old Club started at last and handed over to a Committee to*

manage and I am free. But the amount of writing I have been doing and still am doing is almost stupendous. At any rate I hardly know what it is to go out of doors now. But I've nearly got to the end of it now and then for home!

The Club, which became very popular, was known colloquially as 'The Poultice' because when, at a meeting of chaplains, B-P was criticised for placing it 'among the drinking shops of the town' he replied by asking: 'Well, where *would* you put a poultice?'

As Intelligence Officer for the surrounding countries, to which office he was appointed in August 1890, B-P managed to fit in a good deal of travel amongst his other activities. He visited Albania, Italy, Greece, Turkey, Tunis, Algeria, Bosnia and Herzegovnia, sometimes at his own expense, sometimes at that of the War Office, but generally managing to pay his way by writing and drawing, for the newspapers, descriptions of his journeyings.

A great part of his duties as ADC lay in the arrangement of levées, dinners, balls, concerts, etc. Of his prowess in this direction Lady Smyth later wrote:

He was invaluable in helping to get up and arrange any entertainment, being able, either himself or by finding a friend, to fill up any gap. Notably, once when a lady failed to do her part of the dance on the programme, he donned a lady's dress and, amid roars of laughter, gave a most attractive skirt dance, then quite a new diversion to our audience.

One of his characteristics was that he always seemed to have people able and ready to do what he asked of them, and we seldom had a party when he did not get through 'a lot of business' as he called it, which meant generally that he had booked all or anyone to join in some polo match, acting, dancing, concert, lecture, picnic, etc. etc. which he had on hand.

If Scouts could imitate his continual industry, whether at work or play, and his thoughtfulness and kindness to others, as well as his determination to succeed in anything he attempted, it would go a long way towards making fine men.

Baden-Powell remained in Malta until April 1893 when, on the advice of his old Colonel, Sir Baker Russell, he resigned his appointment as Assistant Military Secretary to rejoin his regiment, the 13th Hussars, then stationed at Ballincollig, County Cork, Ireland.

On 10th April of that year he started for home, paying visits to Tunisia and Algeria, at the request of the War Office, on the way. His first letter home after leaving Malta is dated 26th April 1893 from Souk-el Abra, Tunisia:

Here I am getting homewards by very small degrees for, having got as far as this, I find manoeuvres going on behind me and am just off back again to Tunis and Kairouen. Then I shall make a fresh start and run along the coast to the west end of Algeria. Meantime I am thoroughly enjoying myself and getting together a nice collection of butterflies. I shall be with you by the end of the month in any case.

Eventually, on 9th June, he reached his regiment in Ireland and on this day he wrote:

It is good to be back, everybody so cheery, and I feel quite at home again. In the afternoon the 10th Hussars came over to play us at polo, so I saw them all again, and an enormous crowd of local people came to look on and be tea'd etc. And of course we beat them. My rooms look out into a park of open brilliant green grass, with elm and beech trees. You could never imagine barracks were anywhere here . . . I have taken over command of my old squadron. Tomorrow we leave for Ballincollig. About the 23rd we start for the Curragh for summer manoeuvres.

It was during these manoeuvres at the Curragh that B-P came once more to the notice of Lord Wolseley. He had devised the trick of sending a few mounted men towing branches behind them, which made a big dust that lured the enemy cavalry away, and in their absence B-P popped in with his squadron and captured their artillery. Lord Wolseley, who happened to be watching, commended this use of 'commonsense and cunning' to the assembled officers afterwards, asking for the name of the officer responsible for it.

It was a direct result of this episode that in 1895 he sent for B-P at the War Office and told him that he was going to send him out with the Ashanti Expedition, although it was not a cavalry country—but he had observed that he could use the 'four Cs' necessary for campaigning in that kind of country as elsewhere—Commonsense, Cunning, Courage, and Cheerfulness.

1894 was spent with his regiment at Dundalk and Belfast, during which time he worked at a new edition of *Cavalry Instruction*, a book he had first had published in 1885. In September of that year he acted at the Cavalry manoeuvres at Churn, Berkshire, as brigade major to Colonel French (later Field-Marshal Lord French of Ypres), where another Staff Officer was Douglas Haig (later Field-Marshal Lord Haig of Bermersyde).

8 Ashanti

Crowns and thrones may perish,
Kingdoms rise and wane.

Sabine Baring-Gould

If you look at an old map of the west coast of Africa you may find about half-way down it a spot marked as Cape Coast Castle, Gold Coast. This was the gateway to the great forest country of Ashanti, which was to be the scene of Baden-Powell's next adventure.

The expedition of 1895–6, in which he took part, was the fourth Ashanti campaign within fifty years. In his book *The Downfall of Prempeh,** published after the expedition, B-P told the full story of it and gave as the main objects of the exercise the protection of the loyal tribes and the abolition of slavery and of human sacrifice.

Prempeh, the King of Ashanti, had 'ever since 1874 stood in the way of civilisation, of trade, and of the interests of the people themselves'. At any rate that was the British Government's view of the situation, as voiced by Mr Joseph Chamberlain, the then Colonial Secretary.

In his book B-P stated that:

In England we scarcely realise the extent to which human sacrifice had been carried on in Ashanti. In the first place the name Kumassi (the capital of Ashanti) means 'The death place'. The town possessed no fewer than three places of execution, one for private executions which was at the Palace, a second for public decapitations was on the parade ground; a third for 'fetish sacrifices' was in the sacred

* *Published in 1894: sadly, most of B-P's books are now out of print.*

64

village of Bantama . . . the victims of sacrifices were almost always slaves or prisoners of war.

On 13th November 1895, B-P received his orders to proceed on special service in connection with the proposed expedition to Kumassi, under Sir Francis Scott, and on 23rd November he sailed from Liverpool in the B & ASN SS *Bathurst*. The boat called at Grand Canary and at Sierra Leone, from which place a telegram was sent forward to Cape Coast Castle requesting that a hundred reliable natives might be enrolled for service as scouts. B-P was to command these scouts as part of his native levy, so he occupied himself on the voyage in drawing up a scheme for their organisation.

He had with him in the ship a book about the previous Ashanti expedition of 1874, by Sir William Butler, entitled *The Story of a Failure*. It described how Sir William had raised a native levy amongst the Krobo tribe and organised it with twelve white officers. He took this force up country with the remainder of Lord Wolseley's column but for the attack on Kumassi he was ordered to move by a separate path to outflank the enemy. The day before the battle he found himself, with his twelve officers, deserted by his Krobos.

It was from the experience of this officer that B-P stipulated that his levy should be formed of as many different tribes as possible, so that if one lot mutinied he would still have others on his side.

On 13th December the expedition disembarked at Cape Coast Castle, and B-P got to work on the assembling of his men and the distribution of their various duties.

The assembling of an army of West Coast natives was not so easy a task: the Kings and Chiefs of the country at that time were better at making promises than at carrying them into effect and it required both 'a smile and a stick' to deal with these wobblers.

A parade of 500 men had been promised by noon on 16th December. Here is B-P's account of what actually happened:

December 16th. Noon. The parade ground outside the castle lies in arid desert in the midday sun and the sea breeze wandereth where it listeth. Not a man is there. It is a matter then for a hammock ride

C

through the slums of the slum that forms the town. Kings are forced out of the hovels where they are lodging, at the end of a stick; they in their turn rouse out their captains, and by two o'clock the army is assembled. Then it is a sight for the gods to see Captain Graham (nicknamed 'The Sutler') putting each man in his place . . . If it were not for the depressing heat and the urgency of the work one could sit down and laugh to tears at the absurdity of the thing, but under the circumstances it is a little wearing. But our motto is the West Coast proverb 'Softly, softly, catchee monkey'. In other words 'Don't flurry, patience gains the day'. It was suggested as a maxim for our levy of softly-sneaking scouts but we came to adopt it as our guiding principle, and I do not believe that a man acting on any other principle could have organised a native levy on the West Coast— and live. Gradually out of chaos order comes. Kings and Chiefs are installed as officers, and the men are roughly divided into companies under their orders.

Each man was served out with a red fez with a black tassel. The regiment, after being inspected by HE The Governor and Colonel Sir Francis Scott, moved off on the first stage of its march to Prahsu under B-P's command.

Five days later, B-P and his men had cleared their way through the bush and established themselves in camp at Akusirem, within thirty-five miles of Kumassi. This bush-cutting business of course made progress rather slow and was attended by many difficulties. B-P wrote:

Twisting and turning, now up, now down, clambering over giant tree-roots or splashing through the sucking mud—all in moist and breathless heat, till, tired and dripping, we reach the next site for a camp. Two hours' rest for midday 'chop' [food] and then parade. More delays, more excuses, and at last every man has his tool issued to him, and every company has its work assigned to it. No 1 to clear the bush. No 2 to cut stockade posts. No 3 to cut palm leaf wattle. No 4 to dig stockade holes. No 5 to mount sentries and prevent men hiding in huts; and so on until everyone is at work.

'Hullo, where are the hole-diggers?'

'They have retired to have some chop.'

'*Chop ? They've only just finished two hours of chop.*'

'*Yes, but the white chief works them so hard they have big appetites.*'

'*They—and you, their chief, will all be fined a day's pay.*'

'*Yes, well, the white man is powerful. Still, we prefer that to not having our chop. Many thanks.*'

'*Oh, but you'll have to work as well. See this little instrument ? That's a hunting crop. Come, I'll show you how it can be used. I'll begin on you, my friend.*'

No need to. They all fly to their work. Then you go round. Every company in turn is found sitting down or eye-serving.

'*Down with that tree, my lad. You with the felling axe. Not know how to use it ?*'

For three days I felled trees myself till I found that I could get the tree felled equally well by merely showing the cracker of the hunting crop. The men had loved to see me work. The crop came to be called '*Volapuk*' because it was understood by every tribe. But though often shown it was never used.

The bush-clearing company are sitting down. Not a yard of bush cut. Why ?

'*Oh, we are fishermen by occupation and don't know anything about bush cutting.*'

The bush soon comes down nevertheless, and, what is more wonderful, by sunset there is an open space of some seven or eight acres where this morning there was nothing but a sea of bush jungle. Large palm-thatched sheds have sprung up in regular lines and in the centre stands a nearly finished fort, with its earth rampart bound up by stockade and wattle. Within it are two huts, for hospital and storehouse. Trains of carriers are already arriving with hundreds of boxes of beef and biscuits to be checked, arranged, and stored. At sunset sounds the drum, the treasure box and the ledger are opened, and the command comes up for pay.

'*First Company, how many men present ?*'

'*Sixty-eight, Sir.*'

'*But it has only got fifty-nine on its establishment.*'

'*Next Company ?*'

'*All here, Sir, but some few men away sick—and two he never come.*'

And so on and on. At last it is over except that a despatch runner *comes in with a telegram, forwarded from the last telegraph station, to ask from Cape Coast Castle offices immediate reason why the men's pay list has been sent in in manuscript instead of on Army Form 01729.*

Perhaps the most exciting incident of the expedition was the night march of the flying column to Bekwai.

The King of Bekwai, a tributary of Kumassi, sent messengers to Sir Francis Scott, saying that he wished to come under the British flag, but that protection must be sent at once, as otherwise he would be taken by King Prompeh and executed as a traitor.

It fell to B-P, therefore, to organise a flying column which, cutting its way through the nine miles of bush by night, surrounded Bekwai Palace on the following morning and hoisted the British flag there.

In this night march B-P's force had actually got round the enemy who were in position at Essian Quanta to resist any advance. It was a game of 'hide-and-seek' and the hiders got home. In the morning the enemy found that instead of attacking them in front, where they had expected it, B-P's force was behind them and had cut them off from any help from Bekwai—whom they counted as an ally—and was likely to cut them off from getting back to their main body at Kumassi. So they fled and the road was thus left open for the main British force to come along without opposition. This was really the turning point of the expedition.

This is how B-P described the flag-hoisting ceremony:

African monarchs are hard to hurry, but there was much business to be done, and business on an expedition such as this has to be done quickly. So that, after several messages requesting the King's wishes as to where and when the ceremony of hoisting should take place, I had the staff set up in a spot of my own choosing, paraded my force and sent to tell the King that all was ready. This had the desired effect in the end although the guard of honour of Houssas and of the B-P scouts had some time to wait before the din of drums and horns and the roaring of the crowd told that the royal procession was on the move. Presently it came in sight—a vast black crowd surging and yelling round the biers on which the King and chiefs were borne.

Above and around them twirled the great state umbrellas. In front were bands of drummers with small drums, then dancing men who leaped and whirled along, fetish men in quaint head-dresses, drummers with kettle-drums, trumpeters with their jaw-bedecked ivory horns, and then the great war drums carried shoulder high and hung with skulls which were, however, for this occasion covered with a strip of cloth signifying that it was a peace ceremony. There were the King's court criers with their tiny black and white caps, running before; and behind there rushed the crowd of slave boys carrying their masters' stools upon their heads. The roar and the drumming became intense as the procession came rushing up the road—for it moved at a fast pace—and the umbrellas whirling and leaping gave a great amount of life and bustle to the scene. At last the throne and chair were set and the people marshalled by degrees into some kind of order. I then offered to the King the flag with all its advantages, which the King, with much spirit in his words, eagerly accepted. . . . The King then moved from his seat to the flag-staff. Though it was but a few paces the move involved no small amount of ceremony. The umbrella had to be kept twirling over him while the bearer moved only on the ball of the foot. Men went before to clear every stick and straw from the royal path. The fetish man, in a handsome Red Indian kind of feather head-dress, and a splendid silver belt, appeared to bless the scene. One man supported the King by holding his waist, and was himself similarly supported by two or three others in succession behind. Another mopped the King with a handkerchief, while boys armed with elephants' tails kept off stray flies from the royal presence. The King was dressed in a kind of patchwork toga with a green silk scarf, on his head a small tortoiseshell cap, and on his wrists, among the pendant fetish charms, he wore some splendid bracelets of rough gold nuggets and human teeth.

In all his barbaric splendour the King moved up to the flagstaff. The flag was at the masthead in a ball and as he pulled the halyard that let it fall out in long gaudy folds, the band of the Houssas struck up 'God save the Queen' and the troops presented arms.

The King made a gesture as of going to sleep, with his head on his hand, and said that under that flag he should remain till he died. . . . Later in the day the King and chiefs came in procession and called upon the British officers. This consisted in their filing past, bowing to each officer, and holding his hand out as if to bless him—the greater chiefs shaking hands.

With B-P himself, the King shook hands three or four times over, and even went so far as to dance a few steps—a thing almost unheard of for one of his dignity and intended as a very special compliment to his deliverer.

This all sounds to us like a sort of dream or fairy tale, but it is nevertheless a true description of what took place at Bekwai.

It was not the intention of the flying column to give the King something for nothing. He had to pay for his deliverance by providing men for B-P's army, and after much palaver, and threats on the part of the British to remove his newly gained protection, the King provided a large party of carriers to join the force.

This piece of good scouting had cleared the way for the main body to follow up, and on 17th January the white forces entered Kumassi by the main route while B-P and his levies also entered by side tracks.

Within one month of landing on the Gold Coast, the British were in occupation of Prempeh's capital without bloodshed or disorder. It was then comparatively easy to complete the work in hand.

The story of Prempeh's surrender, of the occupation of his palace, of the capture of the Execution Bowl which had received so many innocent heads, of the total destruction of Bantama, of the horrible discoveries in the execution grounds, and other details which at first seem too gruesome to be possible, were all written down elsewhere by B-P himself as I have said. They are not things to dwell on but it is only by learning of them that we can realise how necessary was this expedition and what good work was thereby accomplished.

The Execution Bowl—an enormous brass bath—was brought home by B-P and lent to the Royal United Services Museum.

The return march to Cape Coast Castle was a more difficult task than the advance on Kumassi, because there was no longer any hope of a fight ahead to buoy the spirits of the weary marchers. They were weighed down with rounds of ammunition which—thanks to the good organisation of the undertaking—had never been required, and they had only themselves and their discomforts to think of.

Fever was rife in that hot airless forest country: B-P attributes his own escape from it to his habit of carrying two shirts, one on his body and the other slung round his neck while on the march. He was thus never without a dry shirt to change into.

Before he sailed, B-P had received a piece of advice from Lord Wolseley as to how to avoid fever. He told him to take to smoking. His dodge was to have a double set of mosquito curtains and after going to bed inside them to smoke a pipe so as to warm up the atmosphere inside and drive out the malaria, which the mosquito curtains would then keep out. In those days it was not known that mosquitoes caused malaria, but these precautions were equally good against mosquitoes.

B-P obediently bought a pipe and some tobacco and used it religiously for two or three nights in Ashanti. But owing to the damp climate the tobacco soon went mouldy, so he threw the whole lot away—and never got fever after all. Neither did he ever take to smoking.

On 5th February soon after daybreak the West Yorkshire Regiment marched into Cape Coast Castle, bringing with them King Prempeh, the old Queen, and their court. The whole party was then embarked for Elmina Fort under escort of native police.

So ended the reign of a cruel King. He lived in banishment until 1924 when he was allowed as a harmless old man to return to Ashanti.

B-P was never forgotten by the men who had served with him in the Ashanti Expedition. Years afterwards in 1923 Captain Rattray, of the Ashanti Civil Service, wrote to him:

The old Ashantis all remember you. You are called 'Kantankye' which means 'He of the big hat'. I cannot understand this for it is a name they gave you long before the Boy Scouts came into being. Can you give any explanation?'

In his reply the Chief Scout explained that he had worn the 'Boss of the Plains' hat (which was what his 'cowboy' hat was known as) long before the Boy Scouts were invented.

For his work on this expedition B-P was promoted Brevet-Lieutenant-Colonel and he had only been back with his own regiment for a few weeks when he was again singled out for special service.

9 Matabeleland

Go where his pickets hide,
Unmask the shapes they take.

Rudyard Kipling

After a few weeks with the 13th in Ireland B-P received the
following letter:

War Office,
28th April 1896

Sir,
Passage to Cape Town having been provided for you in SS
Tantalon Castle, I am directed to request that you will proceed to
Southampton and embark in the above vessel on 2nd May by twelve-
thirty p.m. reporting yourself before embarking to the military staff
officer superintending the embarcation.
  You must not ship more than fifty-five cubic feet.
  I am further to request that you will acknowledge the receipt of this
letter by first post and inform me of any change in your address up to
the date of embarcation.
  You will be in command of the troops on board.

And, as B-P later remarked, in his book on the Matabele Campaign:
'What better invitation can one want. I accepted it with the
greatest pleasure.'
  The Matabele were Zulus under Umzilikatzi who had settled
in Matabeleland early in the nineteenth century, after being driven
out of Zululand by their own King. They had found Matabeleland
to be a country just suited to them and settled there, systematically

C*

raiding the surrounding countries for such cattle and corn as they periodically required.

In 1890 a body of white pioneers had come into Mashonaland under Cecil Rhodes, taken possession there and established their capital at Salisbury. The Matabele King rose to protest, and his consent to the occupation of the white people had to be bought with ammunition and rifles (which came in very useful in their rebellion).

When the Matabele tried to resume their old game of raiding Mashonaland they found police established to drive them out. An expedition against them advanced into Matabeleland, seized Bulawayo and drove out the King who died in exile. Such Matabele as were at home at the time were conquered; but the greater part of them were away raiding in another part of the country and when they returned they were astonished to find their country in the hands of white people and their King dead.

Their astonishment turned to hostility when they found that the white invaders meant to remain in the country, and by 1895 they felt that the time had come to turn them out.

Everything was going badly for the Matabele at that time. First came a drought to destroy the crops ; then a swarm of locusts of a kind they had never seen before ; and last, but not least, came rinderpest to kill all their cattle. All these misfortunes were, of course, attributed to the coming of the white man, and when an opportunity occurred to raise a rebellion and get rid of him the Matabele were quick to seize it.

Through the priests of their god 'The Mlimo' the leaders of the people issued orders that on a certain night, at the new moon, all the men were to arm themselves, and the regiments to assemble in the neighbourhood of Bulawayo, go into the town, and kill every white person they could find. When the work of slaughter was complete they were then to attack the outlying farms and townships and destroy them.

All might have gone well with these plans but for one thing. In their keenness to get the white people cleared out, some of the warriors attacked the farms and homesteads *on their way* to Bulawayo instead of waiting till their return. Although a good many of the inhabitants were murdered, some managed to get away, and among them was a famous naturalist and big game hunter Frederick Selous who, with his wife, rode into Bulawayo and gave warning to the inhabitants. These, to the number of about 1,000 immediately fortified their market hall and formed a rampart round it of a double line of bullock waggons, stocked the place with food and ammunition and organised a defence force among the able-bodied men of the town.

Two nights later the Matabele arrived, to find the place in darkness and all the houses shut up. They suspected that a trap had been laid for them so, instead of attacking they retired outside the town and camped around it on three sides to the number of about 10,000, leaving one side open for the whites to clear out by— once and for all—if they wished to escape with their lives.

Meantime the news of the murdered farmers had got abroad— relief forces marched up to Matabeleland. From Salisbury came a relief column to Bulawayo; and Colonel Plumer (later Field-Marshal Lord Plumer) raised a corps of Mounted Rifles and moved north from the Cape by way of Mafeking. At the same time Colonel Robertson had organised a corps of 'Cape Boys'— natives of Cape Colony.

While these reinforcements were coming up—and it was about two months before they could reach Bulawayo—the inhabitants of the town had organised a field force and were doing their best to beat the enemy off but with only partial success, owing to the difficulties of the situation.

About this time Sir Frederick Carrington was sent for to take command of the troops on the spot and with him, as Chief Staff Officer, went Baden-Powell.

The latter's first letter home from Bulawayo is dated 6th June 1896:

I am getting on splendidly here. Grand climate, most interesting time. I am Chief Staff Officer to Sir F. Carrington and am over-crowded with work, all office work at present, alas. I have all the business of sending off columns to reconnoitre instead of being sent with them. Such is the penalty of my rank. However, I hope the General will himself take the field very shortly and that we shall have at least one good fight.

75

That B-P did not have to wait long for the fulfilment of his desire will be seen in his next letter:

June 7th. I broke my last letter off suddenly because a report just came in of the enemy being near by. Well, of course I got sneaking about to look at him. I was fiddling around all that night more or less, and by daylight was away out in the camp of an outlying column. This lot I got under weigh and sent a message to Bulawayo for all the available troops there to come out and join me—and they came—and we had a grand little fight. 1,500 enemy took up a strongish position in thorny bush, but I went at them with the mounted troops, 200, and instead of stopping to fire when they fired we charged straight into them. It was splendid—they bolted and we followed up for three miles fighting all the time. These Colonials are grand at it, enjoying it all like a lot of boys playing polo.

In a later account of this fight B-P wrote:

We afterwards found out that this impi or regiment was formed of detachments representing all the other impis of the rebels. They had been told by the Mlimo (their god) that the white people in Bulawayo were nearly dead of rinderpest and that they were to come and sit on this rise outside Bulawayo and lure the survivors out to them and that, as soon as the whites attempted to cross the stream, the Mlimo would cause the stream to open and swallow them up. The impi was then to take possession of the town and keep it in good order for Lobengula (their late King) who was about to come to life again. This yarn was most thoroughly believed by the rebels, and when the stream quite failed to swallow us up they became quite dazed with astonishment. That was the sort of belief in which they fought on all occasions. They were fanatics, they believed everything Mlimo told them and this really accounted for much of their courage. On various occasions they attacked us with the greatest bravery in spite of the Maxims and other fire we brought to bear on them; often they attacked right up to the muzzles of the guns, simply because their old Mlimo had told them that our bullets would turn into drops of water on striking them.

Our horses are getting fearfully done up for want of food. However, an instalment of forage arrived to-day and we hope that more things will begin to come up now. You see we are 600 miles from the railway. Rinderpest has killed all the oxen which used to pull the waggons and they are trying to put donkeys to the work; we passed 900 waggons deserted on the road on our way up here; consequently prices are rather high—pint of champagne one pound ten shillings. Eggs thirty seven and six pence per dozen; messing per month twenty pounds for three very bad meals a day without wine or extras.

The difficulties in regard to food supplies for the troops were very great, owing to the lack of transport, and the dual task of getting supplies in and getting the enemy out was a fairly strenuous one.

The long office hours were rather tedious to B-P who was longing for something more active; but it was after all, in Matabeleland that he found his great opportunity of putting into practice his knowledge of scouting. And very valuable this knowledge proved to the conduct of the campaign. He wrote:

Lots of work, chiefly in the office but I have had a few outings and have just returned from a three days' reconnaissance which I have most thoroughly enjoyed. I went with one companion, the very celebrated American scout, Burnham. We went and reconnoitred the enemy's main position in the Matopo Hills—where we shall have to attack them when we get our forces together. At present we have them divided in four columns moving through the country driving off the various regiments of enemy that have been trying to get together; but they are fearfully handicapped, having no food for the animals and very little for the men, rinderpest having killed off all the oxen which served to bring up all supplies for this country and eventually became beef. The country is covered with their carcases and the air is—ugh !

Eggs are forty shillings a dozen, beer two shillings a glass, no milk, even tinned, jam three shillings. We live on bread, jam and coffee chiefly. We have got a nice little house for the General and staff—under the curious system they have here of commandeering. The Government can seize on anything they like, horse, saddle, cart, house, belonging to anybody, use it and pay him a fair price for it. This house looked as if it would suit us and was accordingly commandeered, the owner having two rooms left for himself. It is a grand climate here, neither too hot nor too cold, always fine and such starlight nights. Lots of excitement, enemy near us and seen or fought every day.

July 2nd. I wish we were more out campaigning but as we have to pull the strings in so many directions (this command stretches over 670 miles in a straight line) we have to sit here at the head of the telegraph line. Fortunately the enemy are not far off, even here, and I can ride out any night and have a look at them.

Many of the fugitives from the impis broken up by the British forces in the north made their way down to the Matopo Hills, about twenty-five miles south of Bulawayo, and it became B-P's duty to go down and reconnoitre these mountains. This had to be done by night and it took him about a month of night scouting to find out where the enemy were posted. The Matopo Hills were a very broken bit of country; mountains about 800 feet high consisting of piled-up masses of rock and great big boulders, some of them smooth and dome-shaped, as large as a house, others blocks. These hills were honeycombed with canes and over-grown with bush, and among them the enemy had taken up their position.

On the 26th July B-P wrote from the Matopos:

To-day I've been out eleven hours on a patrol into the enemy's stronghold. It is not the distance that tires one but the constant tension of being on the alert. It is grand fun, very exciting, and so far I have been most lucky and successful. But it is an awful country to fight in and we have not one quarter enough men—but if we had more we could not feed them. I am most thoroughly enjoying myself now that we are in camp and out of the office life of Bulawayo. We have no tents, simply sleep in the open with glorious log fires at our feet and saddles at our heads to keep off the draughts. Of course we never undress (except occasionally to wash) and we turn out every morning before daylight ready for an attack.

Our kit would amuse and astonish you. We are very much like Buffalo Bill's cowboys, no uniform. Even I who ought to show a better example go about in a most ragamuffin but very comfortable kind of dress.

On his night scouting expeditions B-P usually went alone, accompanied only by one reliable native to hold his horse and keep a look-out. He later wrote fully of his many adventures and narrow shaves, and of the value of scouting—that is to say of observation, deduction, keen eyesight, sense of smell, and the Sherlock Holmes methods of putting two and two together.

The Matabele got to know him only too well and named him 'Impeesa'—meaning 'The Wolf that never sleeps'.

Now also his knowledge and practice of the art of skirt-dancing came in most usefully for without it he said he would have been unable to dodge his pursuers successfully and would certainly have been taken prisoner and tortured to death.

Just as the reconnoitring of the Matopos was completed and attacks were being prepared, news came that the rebellion had spread into Mashonaland, that Mashonas were busy murdering farmers and that the towns were hastily going into laager. This was due to a party of Matabele who, after being defeated in a fight, had made their way into Mashonaland and proclaimed the 'news' that all white men had been destroyed, that no Matabele had been killed since their god the Mlimo had turned hostile bullets into water. They therefore advised the Mashonas to rise also in rebellion and to drive the white men out of the country into the sea.

This outbreak of the Mashonas put another 20,000 men into the field against the white forces whose total number in Mashonaland was under 2,000.

Sir Frederick Carrington therefore called for imperial troops from the Cape and columns were immediately sent up.

Meantime attacks against the enemy in the Matopos were proceeding and after about three weeks' fighting, with losses on both sides, the Matabele came out of their hiding-places and surrendered. There still remained forces of the enemy in the north-east and east parts of Matabeleland, and the imperial troops, having arrived on the scene, were sent up to clear these districts. B-P was put in charge of the column of Mounted Infantry and Engineers strengthened by colonials, Boers, and Cape Boys—a very mixed lot but they combined well together.

B-P's next adventure was of a somewhat trying nature as it involved condemning a man to death. He was with his new column and this is his own account of how it happened:

79

The first place we came to was Uwini's stronghold about one hundred miles from Bulawayo. Two impis were immediately to the north of us and another one between us and Bulawayo, so that we were practically working on our own resources. Uwini's stronghold consisted of eight koppies (a koppie being a small mountain of boulders and caves). The column took one of these koppies but had lost one man killed and four wounded in doing so, and they captured one man and this was the Chief, Uwini. Two of our men had very pluckily hunted him about in his own caves—it was like crawling about in a drain—they kept shooting at him and he at them in the dark, until at last he was wounded and captured. Uwini was one of the chief leaders of the rebellion and was supposed by his people to be one of the Chiefs appointed by the Mlimo and therefore immortal. When we got him out I asked him to order his people to surrender but he declined. He said that he had ordered them to kill every white man and to hold out in their strongholds, and he was not going to go back on his order. He was a plucky old fellow but we had no option. He was tried by court-martial, proved to have taken a hand in murdering white people, and was shot in front of the stronghold where all his people could see it. The following day we had a thousand of them in camp: they all gave in. Had we not done this we should probably have lost a number of men in addition to killing a large number of rebels; but the shooting of this one man had the same effect, and we were able to tackle the other rebels to the north of us.

For this shooting of Chief Uwini, the High Commissioner ordered the General Officer Commanding the Forces (Sir Frederick Carrington) to place Colonel Baden-Powell under arrest, for trial by court-martial. This General Carrington refused to do but ordered a Court of Enquiry, which assembled on the 30th September 1896. The Court, having taken all the evidence relative to the case, forwarded their proceedings to the General. This evidence, together with the report of the native commissioner concerned, was ample to show that B-P had been justified in his action.

Sir Frederick Carrington reported as follows:

I am of opinion that the military exigencies of the circumstances in

Right, *B-P at the age of two.*
Below, *at six*

Charterhouse days. Left, *B-P in the school corps, second from left.* Below, *aged seventeen*

In Swaziland 1889 as part of a commission that acknowledged the independence of that nation

In Matabeleland 1896. Because of B-P's bold reconnoitrings among them the Matabele called him **Impeesa**—*'the-wolf-that-never-sleeps'*

'The Hero of Mafeking' in different poses during the siege

Unable to get armoured trains sent from Cape Town before the siege began, B-P had two constructed in the Mafeking railway yard. Here (back to camera) he inspects one of them

A copy of the letter of protest B-P sent to the Boer commander General Snijman after the shelling of the women's laager

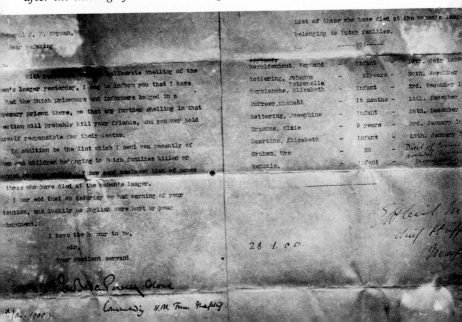

B-P, centre, with his principal officers at Mafeking

'The Wolf', one of the guns made during the siege. It was named after B-P's Matabele nickname

London receives the news. The bulletin 'turned the night into the most tumultuous one in the history of the British capital'

One of the earliest telegrams received by B-P after Mafeking was relieved was this one from Queen Victoria

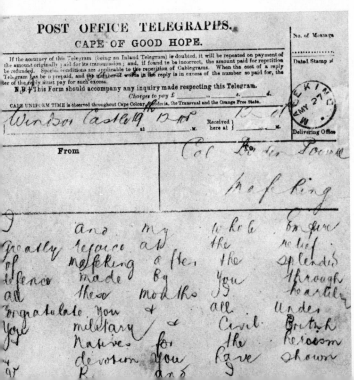

POST OFFICE TELEGRAPHS.
CAPE OF GOOD HOPE.

If the accuracy of this Telegram (being an Inland Telegram) is doubted, it will be repeated on payment of the amount originally paid for its transmission; and, if found to be incorrect, the amount paid for repetition be refunded. Special conditions are applicable to the repetition of Cablegrams. When the cost of a reply Telegram has be n prepaid, and the number of words in the reply is in excess of the number so paid for, the ter of the reply must pay for such excess.

N.B.—This Form should accompany any inquiry made respecting this Telegram.

CABLE UNIFORM TIME is observed throughout Cape Colony, Rhodesia, the Transvaal and the Orange Free State.

The first Scout camp, Brownsea Island 1907. Above, B-P with some of the boys on their way to the Island. Below, outside his tent holding the long, spiral horn of an African koodoo. Each morning he woke the camp by playing notes on this war horn

The family at Gilwell Park 1929. Left to right: *Heather; Lady Baden-Powell, by then the Chief Guide; B-P, who had just received a peerage and took the title Lord Baden-Powell of Gilwell; Betty and Peter. The dog was named 'Shawgm' after the Scouts from Shropshire, Hereford, Worcester, Gloucester and Monmouth who gave him to B-P*

A part of 'Pax Hill', B-P's home in Hampshire where he lived from 1919–39. B-P is on the balcony where he slept out all year round

B-P being proclaimed 'Chief Scout of the World' at the first world Jamboree, Olympia 1920. This title gave him more satisfaction than all of his military ones

Each winter B-P travelled the world meeting and encouraging those connected with Scouting. Here he is in Ceylon 1920 with Scouters

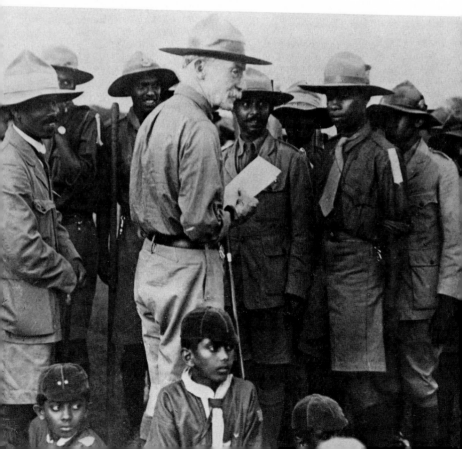

THE MORAL
OF
THE ACORN — AND — THE OAK

May 29 bring luck to you, and if your chances
look but small, remember this – they may expand,
it's not a hopeless thing at all. From tiny atoms
atolls come and acorns grow to mighty trees.
The Scout Plant sown in Brownsea Isle has spread
its branches o'er the seas. In August next it comes
of age, and holds its joyous Jamboree, where boys
from all the world will meet, for you and all the
world to see. This all suggests that if you
make of little steps a big combine you'll get
what most we wish you now —
Success in nineteen twenty nine

Olave Baden-Powell   Robert Baden-Powell

A drawing and message from the Baden-Powells to mark the 21st anniversary of the Movement

In Tangier 1929

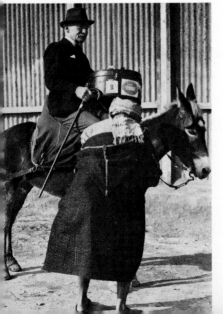

*In America 1929, he was named Chief
Spotted Eagle. Here he is with Chief Joe
Big Plume, the Chief of the Sarcee tribe*

*Being presented with a necklace made of
whale's teeth, Fiji 1935*

Above, *In Melbourne 1935 with Malayan Scouts at the first Jamboree of the Southern Hemisphere.* Below, *visiting the New Zealand section of the camp*

A moment of relaxation in Canada 1935. B-P was a keen fisherman, and the Fly Fishing Association he founded near his Hampshire home in 1920 still exists

At a rally of Indian Scouts in Durban 1936

Chatting to the driver of the bus about to take him to Tilbury en route to South Africa 1937

In India 1937 B-P watched the final of the Kadir Cup, an event he had won fifty-four years previously

In Holland 1937 B-P attended his last Jamboree. 25,000 Scouts from all over the world paid tribute to their Chief for the last time

In January 1941 B-P died and was buried in the shadow of Mount Kenya

*which Lieut-Colonel Baden-Powell found himself at the time of
Uwini's capture were such as to call for strong measures, and sub-
sequent events have, to my mind, clearly proved that the prompt
punishment, at his own stronghold, of Uwini, as a powerful and
notorious instigator of crime and rebellion, exercised a very wholesome
influence on the surrounding district and undoubtedly expedited its
final pacification.*

Another expert on South African affairs, General Sir Henry
Smyth, wrote privately to B-P:

I am real glad that you confirmed the sentence on Uwini, whether
you gain or lose by it, *because it was your duty to do so.*

The case of Uwini and its results is an example of a man carrying
out what he felt to be his duty even when that duty went so far as
condemning a fellow-creature to death. It cannot have been a
pleasant task for any man, and it is a responsibility that few of us
would care to take.
 To his mother B-P wrote:

*Well, on looking back at it I should do exactly the same thing again
(though it sounds brutal, doesn't it?) but it was the means of saving
a large number of white lives as well as of black. We must have gone
on fighting in those caves for days, killing and losing many men
before we could have induced the survivors to give in.*

After Uwini had been shot and his people had surrendered, B-P
moved on with his column into the forest and, by dividing the
column into three strong parties, hunted the enemy about until
they were tired of fighting and came out to surrender. This was not
all done in a day, however, and it was done under extreme difficulties, owing to food shortage and, what was worse, water
shortage.
 The last adventure in which B-P took part, and the one which
practically finished off the Matabele rising, was the capture of
Wedza's stronghold—a large mountain with half a dozen high
peaks on it, each of which was fortified and occupied by the

enemy. B-P found himself not strong enough to attack it and, as he did not like to leave it, played a game of bluff, surrounded it with small posts for two days and a night, kept up a continuous fire from all sides at once and lit up a chain of fires all round it by night so as to give the enemy the impression that he had a big force. This game had the desired effect and after two days the enemy deserted their stronghold and, after being pursued for sixty miles, Wedza and the other chiefs surrendered themselves.

Here is a short extract from a letter written home by B-P on the subject of his attack on Wedza:

After dark we lit a regular chain of watch fires all round the stronghold to make the enemy have some idea of the immensity of our numbers. The enemy attacked our fires once or twice. Jackson, the Native Commissioner, had a narrow escape. He came to me while I was riding round the outposts, when some of the enemy lying hid in the rocks by the path gave us a volley at short range. Jackson was grazed on the shoulder, his horse was shot through the head, and my hat was knocked off. We returned the fire and were immediately joined by the 7th Hussars under Prince Alexander of Teck, who quickly cleared the rebels out. During the night the rebels escaped out of the stronghold into the mountains, which with our tiny numbers we could not prevent.

The effect of the engagement was the taking of a stronghold to which Wezda had invited all rebels to come as it was impregnable. It had in the old days even defied successfully Lobengula. However it is cleared now and the rebels round about are beginning to come in to surrender to the Native Commissioner. . . . I am as well as possible though I must say the two days and night work against Wedza sewed me up for a few hours.

November 14th: At last I have rejoined Sir Frederick after two months' delightful wanderings on patrol with an independent command of my own. We covered some 700 miles of country and had a round of adventure day by day.

In the meantime the imperial troops had arrived in Mashonaland with ammunition and food supplies and had succeeded after some fighting in subduing the rebel chiefs of that country. By 25th

November these had all surrendered and the whole rebellion was at an end.

On 12th December, B-P wrote:

I do believe we are on our way home at last. We hope to catch the Dunvegan Castle *sailing from Cape Town on the 6th January but we have got to get to Cape Town first and there are many slips between cups and lips in this country.*

We leave here (Umtali) tomorrow and hope to reach the Beira railway in three days' time. Then a day will get us to Beira if they give us a special which they will, as Rhodes and the Ladies Grey are going too. Then we go in the Pongola, a dirty little coast steamer, taking three days to Durban, then on to Port Elizabeth, there take the train to Cape Town, where we may be kept a week, talking things over with the High Commissioner.

For his good work in the Matabele Campaign B-P gained a further step in promotion—to Brevet Colonel.

10 Old Places with New Faces

And nearer still and nearer
Doth the red whirlwind come.

Thomas Babington Macaulay

In spite of being fully occupied on service during 1896 B-P had still found it possible to carry on a good deal of writing and sketching work. It was marvellous how he managed to find the time for so much writing and drawing but, as he once said when asked whether he could find time to do a good turn to some Scout Troop: 'No, I can't *find* the time, but when I can't *find* time I *make* it by getting up a bit earlier than usual.'

By 1st March 1897 he had joined his old regiment again, the 13th Hussars, at Marlborough Barracks, Dublin, as a squadron commander. But he had not been there many days before he had been offered, and accepted, the command of the 5th Dragoon Guards in India.

Much as he disliked the idea of leaving the 13th, which had been his home for twenty years, the parting had to come, as he was senior to both the officers above him in the Regiment and he could not have got command of the 13th for seven years.

The news of his appointment at so early an age, to command one of the crack cavalry regiments, was received with delight by his many friends, and letters of congratulation poured in on all sides, both from those under whom he had served and from those who had served under him. He joined the 5th Dragoon Guards at Meerut in April 1897. He wrote home:

Behold me arrived all well and comfortably settled down into my new billet in my old station. It almost feels as if I had been away from it for twelve months instead of twelve years. I am delighted with the Regiment; it is certainly a very fine one and in good condition all round. When I have set things en train I shall run up for a few days to see the Baker Russells at Naini Tal in the hills. . . .

One of B-P's first duties as a new CO was to report to the Inspector-General of Cavalry, who was then at Simla and he did not let any grass grow under his feet in doing so:

It was Saturday evening when I got his note asking to see me and I thought no time like the present. Late in the evening I got leave from the OC Meerut for three days' absence and off I went by the midnight train, reached Kalka at the foot of the Himalayas at ten thirty a.m. Sunday, jumped into the post-cart with the mails, and rattled away up to Simla in six and a half hours, going at a gallop nearly all the way, changing horses every four miles. Splendid scenery, road cut out of the mountain side all the way. Simla very lovely and cool. All Monday I saw the General, and in the evening dined with him. This morning (Tuesday) I left at eight a.m. in post-cart, got out about half-way down the road and hiring a pony rode five miles off to Kasauli where there is a small depot of my Regiment. Then rode on nine miles to Kalka where I am awaiting the midnight train to take me back to Meerut.

B-P found plenty to occupy him during the first few months of his command. An officer who served under him at Meerut wrote:

His great idea was plenty of work to keep off malaria and sickness and in this he was most successful. He also started a Regimental Dairy which gave us good milk. Before he took command fever was rife in the Regiment. He used to work very hard himself.

In addition to the dairy he built a bakery, a soda-water factory, a temperance club, new kitchen on sanitary principles for the officers' mess, and a country week-end regimental camp—all with great success. Even on the march the soda-water factory, bakery and dairy accompanied the regiment. He continued to play in theatricals with great energy. At this time he also exhibited five pictures in the Simla Academy which he afterwards sold for seven guineas apiece!

1898 opened with plenty of work in view:

I find I have a good deal of business on my hands, both the business of pleasure and the business of my duty. I am President of the Dramatic Club of Meerut, I am Secretary of the Pigsticking Club; I have been appointed Acting General commanding a skeleton division which goes out for six days' camping down to Delhi. I am President of the annual big Military Tournament, then comes our annual inspection by the Inspector General of Cavalry—four days' incessant harass.

In April he went on a successful tiger-shooting expedition to Nepal at the invitation of his old CO, Sir Baker Russell, who now held a high command in India.

In August he had two months' leave in Kashmir, and came back with material for many articles, as well as with numbers of sketches—many of which illustrated his book *Indian Memories*.

The cold weather season brought a renewal of sporting activities:

This is our Polo Tournament week and in my old age I am playing for the Regiment. We have three teams entered which shows that polo flourishes amongst us.

Tomorrow the Regiment shoots for the Queen's Cup and I am in the team. Next week we go out for a week's skeleton manoeuvres, the General taking me with him as 'Assistant Critic'. Then I pack up and go myself to Cawnpore to get together three cavalry regiments, which form my brigade, and bring them up, seventeen days' march, to the manoeuvres near Delhi, after three weeks of which I march the 5th DGs away to Sialkote, thirty-seven days' march, settle it there, and then home on leave.

On arrival at Sialkote, B-P turned his attention once more to matters of the comfort, health, and happiness of his men, carrying out the same reforms that he had done at Meerut. The regiment was reported on as the best unit of any arm in India at that time,

which brought great credit on its youthful CO. So it was in the
best of spirits that he left in May for leave to England.

* * *

Meanwhile trouble was brewing in South Africa. Negotiations
between the British and Transvaal Governments had reached an
impasse when B-P arrived in England in that summer of 1899.

At a few days' notice from Lord Wolseley, B-P proceeded to the
Cape with instructions to raise locally a force for employment on
the Bechuanaland and Rhodesian frontier; from which it will be
seen that the British Government were taking no risks; and that
they realised what a war between the Transvaal and Great Britain
might mean.

He sailed from Southampton in the SS *Dunnottar Castle*
('hoping fervently that we shan't be recalled at Madeira').

Before sailing B-P had received definite instructions as to what
he was to do. He was:

*To raise two regiments of mounted rifles and organise local police and
volunteers in such manner as to be available in case of war. The duty
of the force was to be:*
1. *To protect our frontier as far as possible from invasion.*
2. *To keep the native tribes of the north quiet.*
3. *To prevent the Boers from getting possession of such important
   centres as Bulawayo and Mafeking.*
4. *To draw as large a force of Boers as possible away from the
   southern frontier until such time as British reinforcements could
   arrive in Cape Colony and Natal.*
5. *To maintain British prestige.*

These definite instructions guided B-P's actions throughout. The
disposition of his force was left to him to determine according to
local circumstances.

The frontier assigned to him to guard was nearly five hundred
miles long. It was evident that to do any good the force must not
be concentrated in one place, so two independent columns were
organised, one in Rhodesia near Tuli, and the other near Mafeking.

The importance of Mafeking, from the strategical point of view, has not always been realised.

Although a small place with a small population, it had long been the centre of trade and commerce between Cape Colony, Rhodesia, and the North-West Transvaal. It was the great market of those parts and to the more home-keeping Boers, as well as the numerous native tribes of the Northern Protectorates, it was the only known town. It had on that account a very exaggerated value in their eyes.

Mafeking had in the old days been a long-standing bone of contention between Boers and natives till the British finally took it from both.

To the natives of those parts Mafeking was the hub of their little universe and among them the phrase was common that 'who holds Mafeking holds the reins of Africa'.

And the question of which side they are going to take in the war depended on which nation held Mafeking.

In addition to its position as the seat of government of the native districts of the Protectorate, Mafeking was a connecting link between Cape Colony and Rhodesia, Kimberly and Bulawayo. It formed the outpost to either country and an enemy attacking either of them from the Transvaal would first have to crush or to hold the force garrisoning Mafeking, as it would otherwise threaten his communications and rear.

To assist him to raise and organise his force a batch of specially selected officers was sent out to him. Among them were Colonel H. Plumer, who had already made his reputation in the Matabele campaign of 1896 and 1897, and Colonel C. O. Hore who had commanded mounted infantry with great success in Egypt. To these two born leaders of men B-P entrusted the organisation of the Rhodesian and Protectorate regiments respectively. As Chief of Staff he had Lord Edward Cecil, a Major in the Grenadier Guards and a son of the then British Prime Minister.

The period of preparation was an extremely hard one for all; clothing, equipment, supply and transport, ammunition, hospitals, ambulances and veterinary services, all had to be improvised out of the very scanty material available in Mafeking and Bulawayo.

From early in August until the middle of September these

preparations went on for a war which now seemed to be inevitable, and B-P was working day and night to be ready. Everybody, from highest to lowest, worked with such a will that by the end of September everything was ready.

Two regiments had been raised, organised and trained, together with their horses, transport, food supplies, armoured trains, hospitals, etc.

With B-P to the Cape went one companion that had never before been employed on active service—and that was a typewriter. His first letter, typed himself, is dated:

> *In the train, Matabeleland, 11th August 1899*
> *This is my first attempt at typing, my dear Mother, so that you must forgive mistakes. I am on my way down to Mafeking from Bulawayo, a two days' journey, and I took this machine with me as I have a lot of writing to do and I thought the journey would be a good opportunity for learning, and I am playing off my maiden efforts on you, for which I hope you will forgive me. It is, or will be when I get into it a little more, a great success, and quite gets over the difficulty of writing in the train.*

From Bulawayo on 29th August he wrote:

> *Tomorrow I am going to live in camp about three miles out of the town, coming into my office every day. In this way I shall get fresh air, exercise, and save expense. It is very interesting preparing for every game that the Boers may try to play off on us, for all our railway and telegraph lines are laid along their border. So they can cut us off at any moment. Their spies are continually among us. All very healthy and well.*

September was spent in elaborating plans for the defence of the Border. On 22nd September he sent his second typewritten letter to his mother—showing a marked improvement in the manipulation of the machine:

> *In the train again, running up once more to Bulawayo after a very busy time at Mafeking, buying waggons and mules and organising*

the defence of the railway, which runs for the greater part of its length so close along the Border that the Boers have only to run in and blow up the line and run back again to their own ground. Now I am on a short trip to Bulawayo to make sure that all is right and ready there before war begins. After that I shall return to Mafeking and make that my headquarters, as it is nearer to the first scene of action, and is for the moment the most important point of my command.

Up to the end of September he had been organising his forces under the authority of Sir Alfred Milner, the High Commissioner for South Africa, and the Colonial Office; he then held the appointment of Commander-in-Chief of all armed forces in Rhodesia and the Bechuanaland Protectorate. At the end of the month he and his force were transferred to the army which was assembling under the orders of Sir George White, the General Officer Commanding, who had just arrived in Natal from India.

Matters were now reaching a climax. On 2nd October the mule coach with its mails left Mafeking for Johannesburg not to return. On 4th October B-P called out by proclamation the Bechuanaland Rifles and the local volunteer company and gave notice that he assumed command of all armed forces and defences of Mafeking.

During this time he was receiving reliable information as to the moves and numbers of the Boers against him. They were assembling at Zeerust and Lichtenburg in large numbers with several guns, with the avowed intention of breaking up the railways and making a dash for Mafeking, after which they would proceed to take Rhodesia and Kimberley. They were under the command of the old fighting Boer General Piet Cronje.

Baden-Powell now realised that he was in for attack and bombardment. He therefore issued a notice for as many as could to leave the town, and he arranged with the Government for their free passage to Cape Town. (For which he was afterwards asked to pay!)

From Mafeking on 8th October he wrote home:

An army of Boers in three columns, amounting to 6,000 or 7,000 men, are camped within ten miles of us. I have been out during the night scouting round their camps. They are well supplied with guns, etc. We are now awaiting their threatened attack.

When I arrived here from Matabeleland last week the civil population were clamouring for help and getting in a panic. I announced that I was in command and then proceeded to organise all the townspeople into a Defence Force, armed the men and fortified the place. Now we are all as happy as sandboys. I am sending most of the women and children up country in case of the town being shelled. Now I must be off for we have planned a grand attack on the town to practise the defenders at holding it.

On 9th October B-P received a telegram from one of his intelligence officers in the Transvaal: 'Heavy rain expected, look out for your hay.'

This, being decoded, meant 'War is close at hand'. Paul Kruger President of the Transvaal had issued his ultimatum.

On 11th October Colonel Herbert Plumer,* with the northern column, reached Tuli from Bulawayo, and was securely established there. B-P saw that he was likely to be cut off from the outside world, and telegraphed to Colonel Plumer that in the event of communications being cut, he was to assume command of all forces in Rhodesia with the object of threatening the Northern Transvaal, while he, B-P, would do the same from Mafeking, the essential aim being to join hands and work together again when the opportunity arose.

---

* *Later Field-Marshal Viscount Plumer*

11 The South African War 1899–1902

I thank whatever gods there be
For my unconquerable soul.

William Ernest Henley

Here is a copy of the Proclamation giving notice that war had broken out.

Notice by Officer Commanding the Forces
Rhodesia and Bechuanaland Protectorate.

In consequence of the Armed Forces of the South African Republic having committed an overt act of war in invading British territory I give notice that a state of war exists and that the Civil Law is for the time being suspended and that I proclaim Martial Law from this date in the Mafeking District and Bechuanaland Protectorate, by virtue of a Power granted to me by His Excellency the High Commissioner.

R. S. S. Baden-Powell, Colonel.
Commanding Frontier Forces.

Mafeking,
12.10.99

Thus on 13th October B-P and his force found themselves besieged in Mafeking.

During the period of preparation B-P had collected enough supplies to last the Protectorate Force four months. The Cape Government had undertaken to protect the railway with detachments of Cape Police. Plans had been made for forwarding telegrams by inland lines, away from the Border, using despatch riders to bridge the gaps. Homing pigeons had also been obtained to fly with messages from Mafeking. The intelligence officers had prepared good maps of the district.

The armoured train built at Bulawayo and Mafeking consisted of the armoured engine with an armed truck in front and one behind. It carried one Nordenfeldt and one Maxim (machine-guns)—the whole train was, of course, entirely bullet-proof. Defence mines were laid round the town, and on a rise about two or three miles to the south-east where it was expected the Boers would post their artillery.

Lord Edward Cecil organised the boys of the town into a corps of orderlies, thereby releasing a number of able-bodied men for fighting duties. For artillery B-P had one one-pounder Hotchkiss and four miserable little seven-pounders, two of them very old, deficient of sights, and mounted on rickety carriages with unsound wheels: these two 'pop-guns' had been sent up from the Cape in answer to his request for modern artillery. The necessary sights and fittings, new wheels, etc., had to be made in Mafeking, but in a surprisingly short space of time they appeared fit for service.

A special communication railway had been laid for one and a half miles round the north-eastern front of the town for the use of the armoured train and was, of course, for the defence of the town.

For machine guns, in addition to those on the armoured train, B-P had six Maxims and one old Nordenfeldt.

Headquarters was established at Dixon's Hotel in the market square of Mafeking.

His men consisted of approximately 1,000 irregular white troops, 450 in the South African and Cape Police, 390 untrained men in the Town Guard, seventy volunteers, plus 468 armed natives. Opposed to this mere handful were four strong Boer Commandoes with a total of nearly 9,000 armed burghers, who had with them at least seven modern field guns and nine Maxims.

In his staff diary B-P entered a detailed description of Mafeking and its environs:

The town is rectangular, well suited by its position for defence. Open ground all round but commanded slightly by rising ground 3,000 yards south-east.

The valley of the stream south of the town would afford good cover from fire but is full of native houses. The natives being armed would keep the enemy from using it. As an additional safeguard I have established a post in a detached building overlooking the valley. The native stadt south-west of the town prevents an enemy using the valley from that end. Natives (men mostly armed) number about 2,000 to 3,000.

The water-works, one mile north-east of the town, are liable to be cut off, but some good wells exist in the north part of the town and there is a steam pumping station at the railway bridge.

Supplies in the hands of storekeepers are plentiful.

The perimeter of the Defence Works is 10,200 yards (about five-and-a-half miles). On this line we have built thirty-four strong points and linked them up with communication and support trenches where required.

The white population consists of 1,000 males and 437 women and children. The African population numbers about 4,000.

On 13th October the garrison had their first engagement with the Boers. A native brought in a report that the Boers were on the railway, five miles south of the town. The armoured train was sent out from Mafeking, the enemy were shelled and disappeared into the thick bush and rocks.

The same day the station-master reported that two trucks containing dynamite were standing in the yard. Here they were a source of danger to the town so B-P ordered them to be sent north at once by a special engine. Instructions were issued to the driver to push the trucks in front of him, and when he viewed a party of Boers he was to abandon the waggons and return with the engine to Mafeking. The Boers opened fire on the trucks and exploded them. This ruse fairly put the wind up the Boers. They had thought they were attacking two more or less empty trucks. When the dynamite exploded they were terrified and were afterwards ever shy of the armoured train.

On the following day the armoured train again went out to

engage the Boers. The enemy replied with a one-pounder Maxim (pom-pom). The firing was heavy for fifteen minutes and then ceased. B-P fearing for the safety of the armoured train, sent out the reserve squadron to relieve the pressure on the train. Later on a message was received from the train that troops were heavily engaged seven miles out, and reinforcements were wanted. B-P despatched a seven-pounder and one troop to cover the retirement.

The action ceased at ten-thirty a.m. Casualties in the garrison were two men killed, one cyclist despatch rider missing, two officers and thirteen men wounded. Four horses were killed and twelve wounded. This was Mafeking's first casualty list.

The same day a report was received in Mafeking from the police at Maribogo to say that the second armoured train which had been promised to B-P, and which had been delayed at Vryburg, had been captured by the Boers at Kraipan. The engine had been hit with a shell, a twelve-pounder, which burst the boiler.

A letter came in from Piet Cronje, the Boer General, saying that he had nine wounded Britishers in hospital and twenty-two prisoners, all from the armoured train.

On the following day B-P reviewed the fighting of the 14th and recorded:

The men behaved exceedingly well and worked exactly as we have practised except that they forgot the principle which I laid down in standing orders, 'bluff the enemy with show of force as much as you like but don't let yourself get too far out of touch without orders lest you draw others on into difficulties in their efforts to support you.'

The same evening he went round all the defences and warned the people to expect bombardment.

On 16th October the first shrapnel shell was fired into the town. From that time on, during the whole seven months of the siege, Mafeking was bombarded daily, with the exception of Sundays— Sunday being recognised as an armistice-day by both sides.

The same afternoon (16th) at two-fifteen, a flag of truce came in from the Boers, to ask if B-P would surrender to avoid further bloodshed. To this demand he sent back the simple answer— 'Why?'

On 17th October he recorded:

Our water supply has of course been cut off but for some time this will not affect us, as all inhabitants have been warned for some days previously to fill up all cisterns and the railway staff to fill up their tanks, trucks, tenders, etc.

By the time these were exhausted, a home-made water supply was available, made by digging two big wells near the Molopo stream. From these wells water-carts were filled up every night and then posted for the day at convenient points about the town for use of the inhabitants.

B-P recorded:

In the second round of their firing to-day the Boers were ranging and firing on a sham fort I had rigged up outside our lines of defence with a conspicuous flagstaff and flag on it. Ordered another sham fort with dummy gun, flagstaff, etc. to be made 200 yards from Cannon Koppie for exclusive use of enemy.

News had come through that Cronje had got a wholesome respect for Mafeking already, and that he was not prepared to fight truck-loads of dynamite and field mines.

On 20th October B-P received a letter from Cronje, informing him that, as he was unable to take Mafeking without bombardment, he would begin to shell the town on Monday at six a.m.

On 21st October, B-P sent a reply to Cronje's letter saying that he regretted that Cronje could not take Mafeking without bombarding them—but that he was quite at liberty to try that way. He asked Cronje, however, to respect the Red Cross flags, of which there were three, one over the Convent, one over the hospital, and over the women's laager.

On 23rd October, the enemy began shelling the town. Shells were chiefly directed at the Protectorate Regiment's camp, where the wise commander had purposely left all his tents standing to draw the fire, the men being stationed in the trenches and dug-outs. All their horses were in the river-bed and other sheltered spots.

On 31st October, B-P found a treasure in the shape of an old sixteen-pounder.* Instructions were given for this antique to be got into working order and for shot to be moulded for it. On this day two good officers were killed.

At the end of the month B-P reported that the enemy shelling had done little damage to the town, and that casualties so far had been small, but that the perpetual hum of the Mauser rifle bullet was getting on people's nerves.

November opened with the usual bombardment.

B-P devoted most of his time to improving and extending his system of defence. In his staff diary of 1st November is an excellent sketch-map of the fortifications.

The shelling of the town was now becoming more intense and the buildings were suffering but, owing to the fact that most of the houses were built of wood, tin, or wattle, the shells did not do the amount of damage which might have been expected, as they went clean through them instead of blowing them to bits as would have been the case of more solid brick or stone buildings.

On 4th November the town was shelled from five-thirty to six a.m., from nine till eleven, and from two-thirty to five p.m. The garrison suffered only seven casualties, thanks to the system of dug-outs which had been completed.

On 10th November B-P reported that the town was bombarded from a new work the Boers had made at Game Tree, but that most of the shells fell on the dummy fort.

Sunday, 12th November was as usual a day of rest. Cricket matches were held and the band of the Volunteers played at the hospital and women's laager.

At this period the eastern defences were completed and connected up by covered ways.

On 14th November B-P took a census. This showed: Whites, men 1,074, women 229, children 405. Natives: 7,500 all told. Supplies: meat, alive and tinned, 180,000 lb., meal and flour, 188,000 lb.; corn and mealies, 109,100 lb.

White rations required daily were 1,340; native rations 7,000; thus there were 134 days' rations for whites and fifteen days' rations for Africans.

* *It carried the initials B.P. — for Barley Pegg & Co the founders — a curious coincidence.*

The next day Gretje (a nickname given by the garrison to the Boers' biggest gun) fired her three-hundredth shell into the town. In the diary for the 17th B-P entered:

The monotony and strain of trench work and continual call to arms is beginning to tell on men and officers. In the evening sent despatch runner to Kimberley with letters informing them of our situation.

On 18th November the enemy became more aggressive. They advanced their main battery at the south-eastern height about 300 yards, and on the north-west front they pushed their outposts towards the cemetery. These moves were counteracted by the garrison by extending their saps towards the enemy's new works.

On 21st November the town was steadily bombarded from five a.m. till sun-down. A good deal of damage was done to the defence works.

On Sunday, 10th December, sports were held for the towns-people and the garrison, but the band was no longer able to play—a shell having destroyed a number of its instruments.

On Christmas Day, 25th December 1899, by tacit consent of both parties no shots were fired, and both sides kept Christmas Day as a holiday.

On 26th December B-P came to the conclusion that the time had come for the garrison to be a little more offensive. He therefore gave orders for an attack to be made on Game Tree Hill. Some 300 men with guns, Maxims, and the armoured train were employed in the attack. At two a.m. the force paraded, and shortly after dawn the British guns opened fire. The advance was effected with the greatest gallantry, and the whole movement was carried out without a fault. The Boer fort was reached. This was found to be a sunk work with a double tier of loopholes and roofed in. The only entrance was blocked with sand-bags. Here the attackers lost heavily. Having heavily punished the Boers, the force retired with a loss of twenty-four killed and twenty-three wounded.

These serious casualties and increased sickness in the town, due to scanty rations, necessitated the re-organisation of the ambulance services. Three hospitals were established, a general hospital, a convalescent hospital and a hospital for women and children.

On 30th December the difficulty of small change had become acute, and it was impossible to sell less than sixpennyworth of meal because there was no smaller coin. B-P therefore issued special paper notes.

January passed quietly. But in February life in the besieged town became more strenuous. On 1st February Gretje fired her nine-hundredth shell. During this month another count was taken of all provisions and calculations made as to how long they could last. Also there was only forage sufficient for fifteen days and 356 shells left for the artillery. There was sufficient flour, meal, etc., to last the garrison for 105 days, though this only allowed half a pound per head per day. But supplies for the Africans were running short. Horse-soup kitchens had to be established.

Towards the end of the month the garrison pushed their defence works still nearer to the enemy, with the idea of eventually undermining them.

On 23rd February B-P reported:

Our soup kitchen in town is working most successfully. To-day's work with it goes as follows: Half a horse, 250 lbs.; mealie meal, fifteen lbs.; oat husks, seventeen lbs. This made 132 gallons. The soup was of the consistency of porridge. Fifty pounds of above will feed 100 natives.

Another case of starvation occurred to-day making the third that has come to notice.

February 26th. The home-made six in. Howitzer was completed and taken out to fire, but the charge strained the junction of breech and barrel. Another day's work will make it serviceable.

Three new soup-kitchens have started.

On 28th February runners entered the town with despatches. From these it was learned that Kimberley had been relieved on 9th February and this good news put fresh courage into the garrison.

Despatch runners were natives who managed to creep in and out at night through the enemy's outposts with letters. They carried these in little balls covered with the lead paper used for packing tea. These balls were strung together with string and hung down the runner's neck. If in danger of being captured by the enemy he dropped his necklace on the ground, where it looked much like the stones and he had nothing on him to incriminate him. Letters and despatches were all written in a most cheerful strain so that if they fell into the hands of the enemy they would give him a false impression and no inkling of the strain which the garrison was suffering. The runners were paid fifteen pounds every time they got through successfully. But a good many of them were caught and shot by the Boers, so they well deserved their pay.

During the first week of March a new estimate of available food was made. The following scale of rations was decided on: half lb. meat, four oz. meal, two oz. rice or vegetables. Tea, coffee, sugar.

On 16th March the defenders introduced an improved 'loop-hole' for their front line trenches. The loop-holes consisted of steel plates, the opening for the muzzle of the rifle being three inches square. These steel plates were camouflaged and surrounded by sandbags. The Colonial Corps sharp-shooters reported them as excellent. They put a man in each loop-hole. Four of them started singing to a concertina. The Boers, wondering what all this meant, began to look through their own loop-holes. One bold man looked over the parapet. The sharp-shooters killed him.

At this time B-P was informed that he would have to be prepared to hold out until the middle of May. This news was, of course, a blow to all concerned, as everyone had fervently hoped that relief would come long before this.

Shortages now became most apparent. Bank-notes and postage stamps, and coins for currency, had all disappeared, but B-P was equal to the occasion. He himself drew a design for one pound, ten shilling, three shilling and one shilling bank-notes for immediate issue. He also arranged for local postage both for town and Bulawayo.

On 22nd March B-P made the following entry in his staff diary:

Propose to issue one penny stamps for the town, threepenny stamps for fort, one shilling stamps for up and down the country, buying Government stamps and making a surcharge on them.

The proceeds were to go towards paying runners, the expense of whom had mounted up to nearly £400. These runners had been freely used by public and Press, and till then the letters being carried free of charge. But there weren't enough official stamps to go round.

In a letter to his mother dated 30th March B-P wrote:

'You would be amused if you could drop in and see us here. We are quite a little republic and I am a sort of tyrant or president—making my own laws and orders on all points. . . . I have drawn and issued a bank note of my own. . . . Today we are making a new issue of stamps —one with my head on it instead of that of the Queen or of Paul Kruger! That, I think, is the proof of our being an independent republic in Mafeking.'

What had happened was, that realising that his supplies were running short, the postmaster (a Mr J. V. Howat) had consulted Lord Edward Cecil, and he consulted Major Alexander Godley and Captain Greener and the four men decided it would be rather fun to make a stamp of their own for purely town mail—and have B-P's head on it.

Now in his *Lessons from the University of Life* B-P stated that he knew nothing of the matter beforehand, and B-P was quite incapable of telling a lie. Undoubtedly he knew about it only when the first finished sheet of stamps was shown to him, and although he wasn't altogether happy about his own head appearing even if the Queen's couldn't, he was faced with an accomplished fact and indeed at that place and time it couldn't seem of much consequence. It was just an amusing stunt, but it did arouse criticism in some quarters (although none from Her Majesty the Queen). But the photograph of one of the boy cadets was soon substituted for B-P's head.

Years afterwards Major Godley by then General Sir Alexander Godley, KCB, KCMG, who had commanded the western defences of Mafeking throughout the siege, and of whom B-P said in his despatch that he was his right-hand man during the siege, gave me the following information:

I had frequently to go in from my outpost headquarters west of the town to see Colonel Lord Edward Cecil (General Baden-Powell's Chief Staff Officer) and on one occasion when I did so I found the Postmaster with him and they told me that they were going to surcharge the ordinary Government stamps with 'Mafeking Besieged'. As we were always all trying to think of anything that could be done to create interest or amuse or keep up the spirits of the garrison, I of course said at once that I thought this an excellent idea, and one of us—I cannot in the least remember who—suggested that we should have a special stamp of our own, which we all again agreed would be a good idea. This led to a discussion as to what it should be like or what should be on it, and one of us three—I could not say which—said, (more in joke than anything else and solely with the idea of doing something that would amuse the garrison) 'Oh, B-P's head of course!' —and my recollection is that Lord Edward and the Postmaster then arranged to have this done entirely as what would now be called a 'stunt', and as a surprise to B-P and certainly without consulting him. I am quite sure that he never was consulted on the subject and that he was rather horrified when he found that it had been done. I am afraid none of us thought that it might in any way be misinterpreted or even that these special stamps would get abroad, as they were to be issued purely for use in the town.

On 30th March B-P took another census. This showed a grand total of 8,974 souls in Mafeking.

During the end of March the enemy were fairly quiet, in fact, thought B-P, much too quiet. So he stirred up their big gun by occasional shots into the battery from his Hotchkiss.

The total number of casualties incurred during March was sixty-four.

April, the last month of the siege, was perhaps the most strenuous of all. Bombardments were heavier, and on 11th April, thirty high velocity shells were fired into the women's laager, and the hospital was 'pom-pommed'.

On 12th April the following message was received from Her Majesty the Queen:

I continue watching with confident admiration the patient and resolute defence which is so gallantly maintained under your resourceful command. Dated April 1st.

Lord Roberts also telegraphed: 'Hope to relieve you by 18th May.'

Gun ammunition was almost exhausted, only sixty rounds per gun was left. B-P therefore made it known that no guns were to be fired without his orders.

By 15th April the garrison had suffered 389 casualties from shell and rifle fire.

By 20th April the supply of forage had been entirely exhausted and the horses were getting only grazing. But as they were often driven in by enemy fire they were getting into a very low condition, and objections were being raised that owing to their poor condition they would not be fit for sausages. B-P ordered the experiment to be made at once. He visited the sausage factory during the night. It was in full swing on two horses and turning out a very good-looking lot of sausages. It was hoped to do this at the rate of 1,000 lb. a night, using the horses' own guts for skins.

The garrison did not lose heart. New stunts were tried daily.

A traveller in acetylene happened to be in Mafeking when the place was cut off and he had a small supply of it and some jets with him. A big tin reflecting cowl was made with triple lights inside it and B-P had it stuck up on a pole which could be turned by hand in any direction and it gave a strong beam of light. This pole was set up in one fort and shown two or three times in the night. On the following night it appeared in another fort and was then hastily transferred to another. By means of this trick the Boers were induced to think that Mafeking had a regular installation of search-lights and this made them more than ever shy of trying a night attack.

On 23rd April a new acetylene searchlight was tried on the armoured train, 360-candle-power. It was a complete success.

On 23rd April, B-P sent a telegram to Lord Roberts bringing to his notice the good spirit, zeal and pluck of the garrison, after 300 days of siege.

The Boer investing forces were getting anxious and it became a case of now or never. They therefore planned a grand and final attack to take Mafeking. This attack was launched—and defeated

—on 12th May and it is graphically described in B-P's first letter
home after Mafeking's relief:

*I don't know where to begin with a description of my joys, I am like
a spring that has been bent to breaking point and has now been
released. The breaking point was on Saturday the 13th, when at four
a.m. the enemy made their final effort to take Mafeking. Eloff, their
most determined leader, with about thirty French and Germans,
headed the attack and led the Boers straight through our outer line of
defences and into our very midst. But we checked them at our inner
line of defence, so that they could not get into the heart of the place.
We closed our outer line round them, so that when day dawned they
found themselves shut in. Only after nightfall did we finish the job; we
killed and wounded seventy of them, captured Eloff and 108 Boers,
and drove the remainder headlong out of the place. The prisoners told
us that our relief column from the south was getting near. On the 16th
we heard their guns as they fought their way towards us. We pushed
out to meet them and during the night they marched in from the
westward. Next morning I took the whole force out and started
attacking the Boers in their camps and trenches. They did not wait
for more but hurried off as fast as they could go to the Transvaal.
Now we are resting the horses but hard at work relaying railway
and telegraph, and hope within the next two days to be in communication with Bulawayo.*

At three a.m. on the 17th I was awakened by Baden at my
bedside, so you may guess I was very much overjoyed. . . . The end of
the siege has in itself been a grand refreshment to me, it was a long
strain of anxiety and I had to wear a mask of cheerful nonchalance all
the time.*

---

* *'Baden' was of course B-P's brother Major Baden F.S. Baden-Powell
who was a member of the relieving force.*

12 The South African Constabulary

Here where my fresh-turned furrows run
And the deep soil glistened red
I will repair the wrong that was done
To the living and the dead.

Rudyard Kipling

After seven months of hard work by day and night, of daily bombardment, the most meagre of rations, ceaseless anxiety, an empire load of responsibility and complete isolation from the outside world, B-P awoke, as from a dream, to find himself a hero in the eyes of the world.

His promotion to Major-General was the immediate recognition which his services received, and in this connection Lord Wolseley wrote:

I hope you got the announcement of your promotion as early as I sent it to you. You did splendidly and it was indeed one of the pleasantest things I had to do in the war when I recommended, within a few hours of the news being received of Mafeking being relieved, that the Queen should promote you.

You have now the ball at your feet and barring accidents greatness is in front of you. That you may win the goal is earnestly wished for by yours very sincerely, WOLSELEY.

Meantime the news of the relief of Mafeking had of course reached England and the joy that it brought to B-P's mother and

D*

family can be imagined; and not only to those who knew him but to hundreds and thousands of his fellow-subjects who had been watching and waiting for seven long months for the news of Mafeking's relief.

An idea of how the news was received can be seen in a few short extracts from some of the hundreds of letters which B-P and his family received about that time. They came from people of every kind, men, women and children:

I have named my son after yourself, Baden-Powell, as the time for registration is limited I could not ask your permission first.

wrote one enthusiast.

We are going to call our foal after you as we have no baby.

was another decision. Said another small boy:

Dear Baden-Powell, I think you are the hero of the Army. You ought to be plasted all over with medals and made Governor-General of Australia.

A nine year old admirer wrote:

We have two rabbits and one of them stays awake while the other sleeps so we have named him after you as people say you are the man who never sleeps.

Another:

I thought you would like to hear about a little mouse that I have, he is black and white and I have named him after you. I used to have a khaki one who I called General Buller but soon after the reverse on the Modder he sickened with mange and shortly afterwards died. On the day that Mafeking was relieved we gave B-P double rations and ornamented his cage with flags.

To which (and one could go on quoting and quoting) I will add one or two descriptions of Mafeking night in London and else-where:

I can't tell you how pleased I am at Cousin Stevie's relief. Father and I were running about the streets on Friday at half-past twelve simply mad with delight. At the Mansion House the crowd was something terrific, hats flying about all over the place. The illuminations were lovely. The Athenaeum was simply a blaze of gas. We have got three days more at the end of the holidays for Mafeking.

From a village outside Birmingham:

I am writing to you because I thought I should like to write to the Queen's most appreciated soldier. There was such a rush in Birmingham when the news reached us of the relief of Mafeking. People were knocking one another down, they were making such a noise with tins and kettles. In the village the folks bought an old cab for fifteen shillings and set fire to it. First of all they had two drivers and two men for horses to give a man a ride round the green but they upset him. Then they had a sailor to run it round the green several times and they sold the old iron for seven and six by auction.

From another village:

Two little girls are writing to tell you how glad they are that you are free and have got something to eat again. We only knew last night and all the bells began to ring and all the people went mad. We have got a big Union Jack out and nearly every shop has one. A pony had drawers on made of Union Jacks but I don't think he liked it.

That there was in some cases method in all this madness of the rejoicing crowds will be seen by this letter:

On behalf of the students of the University of Edinburgh I forward you the account of a torchlight procession held in honour of your brave son. It may interest you to know that we raised £260 on the occasion, which we forwarded to the Widows and Orphans funds of The Scotsman *newspaper.*

Let us end these quotations with the telegram which Queen Victoria sent to B-P written out in her own hand at the dinner table as soon as the news reached her:

I and my whole Empire greatly rejoice at the relief of Mafeking after the splendid defence made by you through all these months. I heartily congratulate you and all under you, military and civil, British and native, for the heroism and devotion you have shown.

Queen Victoria died less than a year later, but not before a new verb to 'maffick' (meaning to rejoice with hysterical boisterousness) had found its way into the dictionaries.

The despatch of Field-Marshal Lord Roberts, VC, the Commander-in-Chief, British Expeditionary Forces, South Africa, dated 21st June 1900, contained these words:

I feel sure that Her Majesty's Government will agree with me in thinking that the utmost credit is due to Major-General Baden-Powell for his promptness in raising two regiments of Mounted Infantry in Rhodesia, and for the resolution, judgment and resource which he displayed, through the long and trying investment of Mafeking by the Boer forces. The distinction which Major-General Baden-Powell has earned must be shared by his gallant soldiers. No episode in the present war seems more praiseworthy than the long defence of this town by a British garrison, consisting almost entirely of Her Majesty's colonial forces, inferior in numbers and greatly inferior in artillery to the enemy, cut off from communication with Cape Colony and with the hope of relief repeatedly deferred until the supplies of food were almost exhausted.

Inspired by their Commander's example the defenders of Mafeking maintained a never failing confidence and cheerfulness which conduced most materially to the successful issue; they made light of the hardships to which they were exposed, and they withstood the enemy's attacks with an audacity which so disheartened their opponents that except on one occasion, namely 12th May, no serious attempt was made to capture the place by assault. This attempt was repulsed in a manner which showed that the determination and fighting qualities of the garrison remained unimpaired to the last.

While England was preparing to receive the hero of Mafeking with cheers and flag waving, with processions and city freedoms, B-P himself was going on with his next job in the war, which consisted in getting together what forces he could to clear the surrounding country. In these operations he took some nine hundred Boer prisoners and the towns of Zeerust, Ottoshoop, Lichtenburg, and Rustenburg, clearing a tract of country about 250 by 100 miles.

He appointed magistrates over the districts and made Lord Edward Cecil Commissioner over them.

In August he was ordered by Lord Roberts to Cape Town to give to Sir Alfred Milner, the High Commissioner, his views on policing the country. He arrived at the Cape on 7th September, after nine days and nights of railway travelling. The journey was in the nature of a triumphal march, for at every station along the line people collected to cheer him and shake hands, soldiers presented him with their pet pipes and other trophies; and on arrival at Cape Town he was received by the Mayor and Corporation, and the crowd carried him bodily right through the town and deposited him inside Government House.

A little of this sort of kindness goes a long way and though he was now due for some leave to England, B-P saw no chance of getting much peace and quiet in London at that time, so he welcomed the suggestion of the High Commissioner that he should at once raise a police force for South Africa in accordance with the scheme which he had already drawn up.

On 6th June he wrote:

I have got 8,000 of my men in the field now, and doing good work. Everything running splendidly but it does demand a lot of work.

But the same month he was ordered home on sick leave, and while enjoying his well-earned holiday in England and Scotland he received a summons to Balmoral, where King Edward VII was in residence, and he spent there the week-end of 12th October 1901.

On that day he wrote home:

I have just had my interview with the King. Went to his study and had a long sit-down talk alone with him. Then he rang and sent for the

Queen who came in with the little Duke of York, and we had a long chat. . . . The King handed me CB, and South African Medal. It was a very cheery interview and the King asked me to stay till Monday.

At the end of 1901 he returned to the Cape and re-started work with the South African Constabulary. This involved an enormous amount of travelling to inspect his men, as the force was now established in every part of the Transvaal and the Orange Free State. In March 1902 he reported:

Since I've been back I've done 2,000 miles by train and 600 on horseback, on inspection work, and I'm off again tomorrow for more of it in the Eastern Transvaal. . . . I am going to launch out into one expense and that is to give a dinner party to my old Regiment, the 5th DG, who are ordered back to India at the end of this month.

Parting with this regiment had been his one regret in his new successes and that the regret was shared by the Regiment is shown in the letter of a young officer of the 5th Dragoon Guards who, when writing to Mrs Baden-Powell during the war, said:

I can see for myself what our Colonel has done for this regiment. Alas, we shall not see him here again I fear, and I only came to the Regiment to serve under him, so it hits me hard for we shall never get such a CO again.

In June 1902 the war came finally to an end and the country was handed over entirely to B-P's South African Constabulary. Naturally this meant increased work for him but for work he was insatiable.

From June to September most of his time was still taken up in visiting the new police posts which were being formed all over South Africa. In a letter home he wrote:

We generally ride about forty miles a day visiting the farms and posts. Each district constabulary officer accompanies us through his district.

    Lord Milner could not find time to go to Mafeking, but I rode over the night before last, thirty-nine miles, arrived in time for breakfast. The Mayor presented me with a magnificent gold casket.

And in October:

I am just back in Johannesburg from a four days' rush to Durban and back on remount work. Tomorrow I am off to Swaziland.

And so the work went on all through the winter of 1902, work that was very much after his own heart.

In January 1903 the offer was made to B-P of the post of Inspector-General of Cavalry at home. This appointment was, of course, the blue ribbon of the Cavalry service.

Mr Joseph Chamberlain, Secretary of State for the Colonies, was now in South Africa to arrange for the future government of the country, and B-P conducted him through the country and in the tour included a visit to Mafeking.

Then on 30th January 1903 he wrote:

The SAC are giving me a farewell banquet on the 14th and on the 18th I sail for home. I couldn't have wished for a better wind-up for the last three years. To have seen the whole thing, from the very start to this last final incident of Chamberlain's visit and his instructions for the future of the country is a grand and satisfactory experience for me.

From Government House, Ottawa, on 21st April he wrote:

Here we are, after a most successful and enjoyable trip from New York, via Philadelphia, Baltimore, Washington, thence to Richmond, Virginia (John Smith's country). Then, over the battlefields of the Civil War, back to Washington, thence via Buffalo to Niagara Falls and Toronto. Here we are in Ottawa, the guests of Lord Minto. This evening we go on to Montreal, then Quebec, Boston, and New York, home on the Kaiser Wilhelm II, *arriving Plymouth on May 4th. I am so glad I came, this trip has been a great success.*

So he was home again. On 30th May B-P went to Cardiff to be

made a Freeman of that City, amongst the cheers of a hundred thousand citizens.

In August he was in Ireland for manoeuvres. In September he visited Dresden as the guest of the King, to be present at the review of the Army Corps, also visiting the Cavalry Schools at Saumer and Vienna, and spending Christmas at Mentone.

1904 and 1905 saw two big developments in the Cavalry under the new Inspector-General. He founded the Cavalry School at Netheravon and inaugurated the Cavalry Journal, to stimulate interest and develop and ventilate new ideas in that branch of the Service.

Duirng these last few strenuous years, B-P had had little time for his usual hobbies and sport, but in July 1904 he did have some successful salmon fishing.

In September he visited the French Cavalry manoeuvres at Bar le Duc. Early in 1905 he visited the Italian Cavalry Schools at Tor di Quinto and Pinerolo.

The Duke of Connaught had, in March 1904, been appointed Inspector-General of the Forces, so B-P found himself again serving in close connection with his Royal Highness who had always followed his work with interest and approval. When the Duke's duties took him to South Africa in the autumn of 1905, B-P accompanied him in his capacity of Inspector-General of Cavalry, so in January 1906 he arrived once more at the Cape.

The same year he visited the Belgian Cavalry at Brussels and early in 1907 made a trip to Egypt. From Luxor he wrote:

I have had three days here and seen all the wonderful ruined temples at Luxor, Carnac, and Thebes, and the tombs of the Kings of Egypt.
All these I had of course read about and know them well from paintings and photographs but to meet them face to face has been a very new sensation, and I thoroughly enjoyed it.

This year, in addition to publishing his delightful book of *Sketches in Mafeking and East Africa*, B-P exhibited 125 drawings at the Bruton Gallery, and also a bust of Captain John Smith in the Royal Academy Exhibition.

1907 saw the completion of his term as Inspector-General of

Cavalry, and it also saw the dawn of the Boy Scout Movement.

Colonel Tom Marchant, DSO, who later commanded the 5th Dragoon Guards, gave this interesting sketch of B-P at this time:

I was ADC to him for two years while he was Inspector-General of Cavalry in England. It was at about the end of that time that he began the Boy Scout Movement. He always took the greatest interest in children and would play with them by the hour. His energy as I-G Cavalry at once became apparent, for whereas in the past it had been customary for each regiment to be inspected once a year, he visited and inspected regiments twice or three times in that period. It was while he held this appointment that the Cavalry School was established for the instruction of junior officers and selected NCOs in the higher branches of equitation. He it was who introduced the idea and organised it on similar lines to those already in existence on the Continent, having paid visits of inspection to the Cavalry Schools of France, Italy and Austria while carrying out his plan.

He was in favour of officers devising new methods for training their men individually rather than keeping too closely to the drill book, because it made them think about their profession. With this object in view he encouraged young officers, when he inspected their troops at individual training, to show him methods and competitions devised by themselves to instruct and at the same time to interest their men.

As might be expected these devices were not always good, in fact some were poor; but when questioned on this point he said that they had at any rate been made to think.

At this time it was wonderful to see the popularity of the hero of Mafeking: wherever he went thousands turned out to see him, and often it was almost impossible to leave railway stations on account of the crowds which waited to catch a glimpse of him.

In Glasgow, on the occasion of an inspection by him of the Boys' Brigade, the crowd broke through the barriers, pressing round him, patting his horse, and cheering him to the echo; and it was with difficulty that he was conducted from the parade ground by a troop of cavalry, the pressure of the people was so great.

13 A Second Life

Teach us to rule ourselves always
Controlled and cleanly night and day;
That we may bring if need arise,
No maimed or worthless sacrifice.

Rudyard Kipling

The Scheme of Scouting for Boys did not take shape all in a day. It had been gradually evolving in B-P's mind since he first had men to command, in those early days in India with the 13th Hussars. He had realised then that the ordinary training of soldiers was not practical and gave them no scope for initiative in war, nor character for making a success of civil life later on.

In the 13th Hussars, the 5th Dragoon Guards, and in the South African Constabulary he had experimented with what is known as 'scout' training with the men under him; and in Mafeking he had seen how this training was equally applicable to boys if they were trusted and put on their honour.

On his return from South Africa after the Boer war, B-P found that his book *Aids to Scouting* was being used in boys' schools and in girls' schools also. Since this book, first published in 1899, had been written for soldiers he began to turn the matter over in his mind and find out what it was in it that appealed so strongly to children, and he then set to work to re-write it as a book for boys.

In 1906 B-P sent an outline of his scheme of *Scouting for Boys* to the leading members of boys' Movements, and many prominent personalities in the Army, the Navy, the Church and the State, and the replies and comments which he received were all so encouraging that he decided to go on with it.

Lord Roberts was one of the first to express approval of the scheme:

I like the idea and think it may have good results. Boys are very receptive and would enjoy the delights of such training if it were carried out in a satisfactory manner. Good instructors would be needed and I suppose a certain amount of financial assistance would be required. I am sure it would be better for the boys to spend a day in bicycling in the country near the large towns, and learning to scout than to waste their time—as so many of them do—in looking on at games in which they are not sufficiently skilled to take part themselves. I hope your scheme may be given a fair trial.

When the Boy Scout Council was formed some years later, Lord Roberts was one of its first members.

In 1907 B-P lectured on his Scouting scheme in many large towns and the same year he conducted the now famous experimental trial Scout camp at Brownsea Island, Dorset. Here he set boys to work, for the first time, under the Scout Law, and what is now so well known as the 'Patrol System', i.e. boys working under a boy leader. The boys had a glorious time and rose above even the expectations that B-P had of them; the experiment was an undoubted success.

1908 opened with the publication of the famous hand-book *Scouting for Boys*, which appeared in fortnightly parts before it took book form. Before the series was half completed, Troops of Scouts had sprung up like mushrooms all over the kingdom. With the help of the late Mr C. Arthur Pearson (later Sir Arthur), B-P was able to get his scheme into working order and to start a weekly boys' paper *The Scout* in order to keep in touch with his youthful band of followers who were now looking to him for a lead. These were not only in England for the Scouting fever had spread to other countries and other parts of the Empire as well and the game of Scouting was demanding guidance and administration.

The uniform of shirt, shorts, scarf and wide-brimmed hat was that which B-P himself had worn on service and which he had found more serviceable than anything else. The South African

Constabulary had adopted it and it became automatically the uniform of the first Boy Scouts since it was in that that B-P was best known to his hero-worshippers.

Still in the Army, he was at that time in command of a Northumbrian Territorial Division, so that it was only his spare time that he could devote to the boys who looked on him as their leader.

1909 saw the first big Rally of Boy Scouts, which was held at the Crystal Palace and attended by 11,000 boys. Scotland was not far behind and they held a Rally the same year at Glasgow, when 6,000 Scouts wearing the kilt instead of shorts, gathered to meet the Chief. A new book *Scouting Games* from B-P's pen was forthcoming that year. Another training camp was held at Buckler's Hard and on the naval training ship *Mercury*, where Sea Scouting may be said to have been inaugurated.

That same year B-P was knighted by King Edward. Writing from Balmoral Castle on Sunday, 3rd October, he said:

I came on here this morning by the King's mail train to Ballater. Royal carriage and pair met me there and here I am. I have had a long walk and talk with Mr Haldane and am to see the King presently when I have dressed for dinner. Haldane* has hinted to me that the King is going to make me KCVO.

P.S. later. Just before dinner the King sent for me. The Equerry, Colonel Legge, took me to his (the King's) room, and while outside the door took off my miniature medals and pinned two safety-pins on the outside of my coat and ordered a footman to take in a cushion. It was like preparation for an execution! Then we walked in. The King in Highland costume shook hands and told me that for all my past services, and especially my present one of raising Boy Scouts for the country he proposed to make me Knight Commander of the Royal Victorian Order. Then he sat down and I knelt in front of him, the equerry handed him the sword, he tapped me on each shoulder, then hung the cross round my neck and hooked the star of the Order on my coat and gave me his hand to kiss, and then told me that his valet would put the ribbon right for me—and off I went. Then after dinner he called me up and asked me all about the Scouts and talked about

* The then Secretary of State for War.

them for half an hour, and suggested that I should bring them to Windsor Park for him to see in the summer.

In this conversation the King cordially agreed to the suggestion that Scouts who proved themselves exceptionally good should receive the title of 'King's Scouts'.

In 1910 B-P had realised that if the Scout brotherhood were to develop on the lines which he had worked out (it already numbered 123,000) it must become for him a full-time job. King Edward was of the same opinion. They both felt that even if it might mean the end of his own career he could do more for his country by training the rising generation to be good citizens than by training a handful of men for possible future fighting.

So after more than thirty years of soldiering, during which he had drunk to the brim of adventure, hard work and well-earned honour, B-P retired on to the Reserve with a reward for good service, a brilliant past to look back upon, and still young enough to embark on what he described as his 'second life'.

King Edward had been one of the first to see possibilities in the Scout Movement and his death in 1910 was a great sorrow to B-P.

The life of a cavalry officer and the life of a Chief Scout of a Movement with its aim of world-wide peace and brotherhood would seem at first sight to have little in common. But look again.

'Train your scouts as individuals and then harness that individuality for the good of the whole' had always been one of B-P's maxims and this was as applicable to boys as to men. During his soldiering career he had fitted himself by practice in leading men, by travel, hard work and experience, to be a leader of youth; and having seen at first hand so much of the horrors of war he was in a good position to promote peace.

It was at first urged that with a General at the head and so many military titles at the top the Scouts could not be other than military. B-P's reply to this was that there was no reason why an old circus horse, having finished his career in the ring, should not settle down contentedly to the useful civil occupation of pulling a baker's cart.

Party politics never had any attraction for B-P. When, after the South African war, he was invited to stand for Parliament he could not resist sending this reply to Lord Roberts' telegram: 'Delighted—which side?'

A free man at last he set himself enough work to keep him more than busy for the rest of his life.

He went off to Canada in 1912, where Scouting had been keenly taken up and was in need of some help in organisation. He took with him two Patrols of typical Scouts selected by competition from Troops at home. These Scouts toured Canada, giving demonstrations of pioneering, tracking, camping, cooking, and other Scouting activities, to illustrate the lectures which B-P gave in the principal centres. America, also, was biting at Scouting—and the story of how they came to adopt the training should not be forgotten.

A rich American publisher, Mr William D. Boyce, was walking in London and was lost in a fog, when a boy came up to him and offered to direct him and to carry his bag. To the American's astonishment he flatly refused to accept any reward for doing so, explaining that he was a Boy Scout, and did not accept tips. On thinking it over the American came to the conclusion that there must be something in the spirit of a Movement which made an obviously poor boy refuse what would be to him a handsome sum of money. He bought a copy of *Scouting for Boys* and returned to America determined that America should have Scouting too.

Scouting for Boys continued to have an extraordinary reception not only in the British Empire and in America, but from countries everywhere came applications for permission to translate and publish for their boys.

1911 saw B-P appointed Hon. Colonel of his original Regiment, the 13th Hussars (later the 13/18th Royal Hussars Queen Mary's Own); and the same year marked a big step in the Scout Movement. The new King, George V, inspected the greatest gathering of boys ever seen, 33,000 Scouts, in Windsor Great Park.

14 Pax

For a happier lot
Than God gaveth me
It never hath been
Nor ever shall be.

Robert Bridges

From this time forward B-P's life became very largely a history of the Scout Movement. But a few personal details must be added to bring our story, which is largely concerned with the first of his 'two lives' to a close.

It was on board the *Arcadian*, bound for the West Indies in 1912, that he met his future wife, Miss Olave Soames, and his marriage to her that same year has been described as B-P's greatest stroke of genius. For he married the one person of all others who could help him in what threatened to become an overwhelmingly large task.

As fresh needs arose, fresh ideas were forthcoming to meet them. Girl Guides for the would-be Scout sisters; Wolf Cubs for the younger brothers who did not like being left out of the game; Sea Scouts for boys with a seaward bent; Rover Scouts a form of Scouting for the older boys and young men returning from the First World War; training courses for Scoutmasters; and badges for proficiency in every subject which could interest a boy.

To keep pace with such a Movement meant much hard work as well as genius, and this was where Lady Baden-Powell, with her youthful energy, charm, and belief in the possibilities of both Scout and Guide branches, was able to do so much to help him.

When B-P took the boys in hand he was apt to find, amongst

his Scout Troops on parade, various small girls dressed in the nearest approach they could make to Scout uniform and clamouring to be Scouts like their brothers.

The outcome of this enthusiasm was that, with the help of his sister Agnes, B-P had written a handbook for girls and devised for them a scheme which, while giving them the same Promise, Law, and ideals as the Scouts, directed their energies into channels which would give them a useful home training camouflaged by means of uniform, badges, games, and the spirit of adventure.

When B-P married in 1912, the Guides had hardly begun, and were soon to need strong and imaginative leadership which could adapt his principles to girls without making 'tomboys' or imitation Scouts of them.

Lady Baden-Powell became Guide Commissioner for Sussex in 1916; in 1917 she was appointed Chief Commissioner; and by 1918 she had won for herself, by sheer hard work, by tact in dealing with those who had been longer in the Guide Movement, and by the charm and energy I have mentioned, the title of Chief Guide.

To B-P and his wife three children were born, Peter* in 1913, Heather in 1915, and Betty in 1917. On Armistice Day in 1918 the B-Ps found a home at Bentley in Hampshire, and changed its name from Blackacre to Pax Hill to commemorate the end of the First World War and to emphasise the spirit of Scouting.

From this house, for the next twenty years, they were to direct and inspire his twin Movements, and to lead them into the many countries where they exist today.

In 1920, at Olympia, London, the first World Jamboree, or international rally was held. (On this occasion the visiting Scouts camped in Richmond Park. Since that time jamborees have been international Scout camps.) B-P was then and there awarded the title which satisfied him more than any of his military ones: he was acclaimed 'Chief Scout of the World'.

Four years later, at the World Camp of the Guides at Foxlease, Lady B-P was appointed 'World Chief Guide'.

B-P's mother died during the First World War. His message to the Scouts at this time will tell how much she had been to him:

* *Peter succeeded his father as Lord Baden-Powell. The present (third) Lord Baden-Powell is Peter's son, and B-P's grandson, Robert.*

Most Scouts know what it is to have a good mother, and the more they like her the more they dread the idea of losing her. Your mother has done so much for you in having all the pain and trouble of bringing you up as a child—in health and in sickness, steadily working to pull you through. She has taught you and watched over you with anxious eyes. She has given up all her time and love to you. When she dies you feel it a terrible blow, the breaking of a happy tie.

I have just lost my mother after some fifty years of loving comradeship; so I know what it means.

She had trained me as a boy; she had watched every step of my work as a man. When I first had the idea of starting Boy Scouts I was afraid there was not so much in it as I had thought, until she spoke to me of it and showed that I might do good to thousands of boys if only I stuck to it. So I did.

BUT IT WAS THANKS TO HER THAT THE SCOUT MOVEMENT STARTED AND WENT ON.

Many Scouts seem to have thought of this on hearing of her death, for I have had a number of kind messages of sympathy from them, as well as a beautiful design of flowers with the motto 'Be Prepared' from the Boy Scouts' Association. For all these kindly tributes I offer my heartfelt thanks. I only pray that those who have been so good to me will, in their turn, find comfort when the dark day comes of their own mother's death.

There is only one pain greater than that of losing your mother, and that is for your mother to lose you—I do not mean by death but by your own misdeeds. Has it ever struck you what it means to your mother if you turn out a 'wrong 'un' or a waster? She who taught you your first steps, your prayers, your straight ideas, and was glad when you showed that you could do things.

As she watched you get bigger and stronger and grow clever, she had hoped in her heart of hearts that you were going to make a successful career, and make a good name for yourself—something to be proud of.

But if you begin to loaf about and do not show grit and keenness, if you become a slacker, her heart grows cold with disappointment and sorrow—though she may not show it; all her loving work and expectation have been thrown away, and the pain she suffers by seeing you slide off into the wrong road is worse than if she had seen you lost in death.

You have not the power of preventing her from losing you by death, but you can save her from losing you in this other way.

Make your career a success, whatever line you take up, and you will rejoice her heart. Try not to disappoint her but to make her happy in any way you can; you owe it to her; and when she dies it will be your greatest comfort to think that at any rate you did your best for her and tried to be a credit to her while she lived.

I never knew a really good manly fellow who was not also a good son to his mother; and by acting up to his mother's expectations many a man has raised himself to the top of the tree.

With the European war had come the first great test for the Scout Movement. The Boy Scouts went into camp in 1914, according to their usual custom for what was then the August Bank Holiday week-end. Thus, when war broke out on 4th August, they were ready, to the number of 50,000, to assist the civil and military forces should their services be required.

The Home Office, Post Office, War Office, and Admiralty made immediate use of B-P's offer of the boys' services. Scouts were used in large numbers to guard the telephone wires from the big naval ports. From the War Office hourly demands were made for their services as messengers, orderlies at the headquarters of the chief Commands and as despatch runners.

From Lord Kitchener came the first request for Scouts to be placed on the coast, as the Admiralty had withdrawn the coast-guards for service afloat and the coast of England and Scotland was unguarded and unwatched. This service was maintained during the whole of the war period, records showing that 23,000 Scouts did their turn at this coast-watching duty, which work was performed to the entire satisfaction of the authorities.

Mr David Lloyd George, the then Prime Minister, wrote of them:

I do not think I am exaggerating when I say that the young boyhood of the country, represented by the Boy Scouts' Association, shares the laurels for having been prepared with the old trusted and tried

British Army and Navy. For both proved their title to make this claim when the Great War broke upon us like a thief in the night. It is no small matter to be proud of that the Association was able, within a month of the outbreak of war, to give the most energetic and intelligent help in all kinds of service. When the boyhood of a nation can give such practical proof of its honour, straightness, and loyalty, there is not much danger of that nation going under, for these boys are in training to render service to their country as leaders in all walks of life in the future.

Year by year the twin Movements continued to grow in numbers and popularity. It was the romance of Scouting that had attracted its first adherents; and that is what will continue to draw boys—and girls—into the Movements so long as they remain true to the Founder's scheme; for though times and conditions change, young people remain in essence much the same as when B-P wrote this, more than fifty years ago:

Where is there a boy, even in these materialistic times, to whom the call of the wild and the open road does not appeal? Maybe it is the primitive instinct, anyway it is there. With that key a great door may be unlocked, if it is only to admit fresh air and sunshine into lives that were otherwise grey.

The heroes of the wild, the frontiersmen and explorers, the rovers of the seas, the airmen of the clouds, are pied pipers to the boys. Where they lead the boys will follow and these will dance to their tune when it sings the song of manliness and pluck, of adventure and high endeavours of efficiency and skill, of cheerful sacrifice of self for others. There's meat in this for the boy; there's soul in it.

Watch that lad going down the street; his eyes are looking far out. Is his vision across the prairie or over the grey-backed seas? At any rate it isn't here.

Have you never seen buffaloes roaming in Kensington Gardens, past that very spot where Gil Blas met the robbers behind the trees? And can't you see the smoke from the Sioux lodges under the shadow of the Albert Memorial? I have seen them there these fifty years.

Through Scouting the boy has the chance to deck himself in frontier kit as one of the great brotherhood of backwoodsmen. He can track and follow sign; he can signal, he can light his fire and build his shack and cook his grub. He can turn his hand to many things in pioneering and camp-craft.

His unit is a band of six, commanded by their own boy leader. Here's the natural gang of the boy whether for good or for mischief. Here's responsibility and self-discipline for the individual. Here's esprit de corps for the honour of the patrol as strong as any house spirit in a public school.

The 'Coming of Age' Jamboree at Arrowe Park, Birkenhead, was the biggest thing that had till then happened in the Scout world. Amongst the many gifts which B-P received on this occasion was a Peerage, but he also received from the Scouts of the world a Rolls-Royce with a trailer caravan for his camping expeditions. Subscriptions towards this had been limited to one penny per Scout so the car became known as the Penny Jam Roll and the Eccles caravan as the Eccles Cake—a confection very popular in the north of England. There was also a portrait of himself by Mr David Jagger, and a pair of braces from the Scouts of the Irish Free State. And thereby hangs a tale. When it was rumoured that there was a present in the offing, Lady Baden-Powell was asked to find out quietly what would please him most and, coming into the study one morning, she asked him whether there was anything at all that he needed. B-P's unsuspecting reply was that he was not in need of anything except a new pair of braces. The story got round and the braces were presented with due ceremony at the Jamboree.

Gilwell Park, the house on the border of Epping Forest, which had been found during the war years and presented to the Movement by Mr W. F. de Bois Maclaren, a Scottish Commissioner, and opened in 1919 as a training camp for Scoutmasters, was now a flourishing international centre for training leaders of the Movement; and B-P decided to take the title of Gilwell when the peerage was conferred on him. Much as he loved Pax Hill he foresaw that the house might in future pass out of the hands of the family—which indeed it did—while Gilwell was likely to last as long as there were any Scouts; so he became Lord Baden-Powell of Gilwell, an honour which he accepted for the sake of the

Scout Movement after much persuasion from his followers. He wanted no such honours for himself.

During those happy twenty years at Pax Hill the Scout and Guide Movements may be said to have grown up. The spring and summer usually found the B-Ps at home but each winter they toured the world—visiting the Scouts and Guides in India, Australasia, South Africa, or wherever the need for their presence was greatest, for now not only their homeland but the world at large was their responsibility. They were in demand everywhere for Rallies and Jamborees, and were received everywhere as VIPs.

When at home at Pax Hill, however, B-P continued to lead the simple life which he loved, sleeping out of doors in all weathers and getting up at five o'clock for an early walk before settling down to his desk.

Though the world was his parish he left his mark also on the neighbourhood round his home. The 'Open Book' sign which stands at the cross-roads in Bentley village was carved and painted by Scouts to his design. The stretch of the river Wey where, on summer evenings, he wandered with rod and line—more for the sake of the scenery and air than for the fishing—became 'The B-P Fly Fishing Association'. And each year, when in England, he carried his knife, fork and spoon to the ex-servicemen's dinner in the village hall, in the re-building of which—as a war memorial—he had taken a large share.

Busy as he always was with his own Movement, a great deal of work fell to his lot in other directions too. He continued to work for his old Regiments, the 13th Hussars and the 5th Dragoon Guards. From his first day of joining the 13th Hussars (in 1876) until in 1937 he attended their last mounted parade in India, on the eve of the Regiment's mechanisation, nothing was too much trouble that could in any way help to maintain the morale and great tradition of the Regiment. One of his pleasant duties was to interview the young men who sought commissions therein and over this he took the greatest care and interest.

He had founded the *Cavalry Journal* and continued to write and draw for it. His old school, Charterhouse, claimed quite a lot of his time; as did the survivors of the Mafeking Siege and Relief forces, who had their annual reunions in London and, later, at Pax Hill. The South African Constabulary also had its reunion each October when the old hands came together to meet him.

Another interest which took him to London at least once each week, was the Mercers' Company, of which he was Master in 1914 and whose Courts he attended regularly. This beneficent Company had given immense help to the Scout Movement in its financial appeals, also had in its gift certain pensions for old people, and when one of these came B-P's way he took great trouble in the selection of beneficiaries. His care and concern for these old ladies were no less than he gave to the young men for the Regiment.

Another great interest, though latterly he seldom managed to attend its meetings, was the London Sketch Club where—if it had not been for Scouting and Guiding—he would have spent a great deal of time. He was a good black and white artist as well as a water colourist and enjoyed nothing better than meeting his fellow artists and learning from them. He had exhibited sculpture at the Royal Academy and was a regular contributor to the Officers' Art Exhibition and to his local show at Alton.

B-P had now reached the top of the tree in each of two separate lives—that of an Army officer, and that of Chief Scout—and he was preparing for a third life—that of retirement, in which he hoped to do some of the many things for which he had never had time.

In 1937 he attended his last World Jamboree, at Bloemendaal in Holland. On the opening day, 31st July, he stood beside the Queen of the Netherlands while twenty-five thousand Scouts from thirty-one countries marched past Her Majesty. The Queen, with her daughter-in-law Princess Juliana, later Queen Juliana, and her son-in-law Prince Bernhardt, himself an enthusiastic Scout, were present on many occasions during a wonderful fortnight.

But B-P was growing old and realised that the time for retirement had come. As he spoke his farewell message to the thousands of Scouts his voice was charged with emotion:

The time has come for me to say Good-Bye. You know that many of us will never meet again in this world. I am in my eighty-first year and am nearing the end of my life. Most of you are at the beginning and I want your lives to be happy and successful. You can make them so by doing your best to carry out the Scout Law all your days, whatever your station and wherever you may be.

Africa had been the scene of so much of B-P's early life and adventure and now, in his last years, he longed to be back in its sunshine. He loved the open spaces and wide views of the land into which two of his three children had married and were bringing up their families.

He had had a little bungalow built in the grounds of the Outspan Hotel at Nyeri in Kenya and there he and his wife spent the next three years, and he was at last able to draw, paint, write and fish to his heart's content. He also loved to visit 'Treetops', near by, from which elephant and rhino could be watched at their feeding place, and at other times to stalk the wild animals with his cine-camera.

In 1940 he wrote of a typical outing:

So we started off, Olave and I, with two servants in the car, away across the great grass plain which lay for thirty miles between us and Mount Kenya. Within five miles of our green lawns and bright gardens at Nyeri we came on the dried-up sunburnt country which the rains had not touched.

For mile after mile we motored slowly across open undulating plains, with never a kraal or a tree and only occasionally scrub bushes. Why slowly? Because every few yards we had to stop and look at the wild game getting such grazing as they could from the withered grass. Zebra were there in hundreds, their fat round rumps showing that though the country looked bare there was still sustenance in it. 'Tommies'—that is the smart little Thomson's gazelles—were everywhere and not at all afraid of our car. Hartebeests in plenty, looking almost like so many chestnut horses with their heads stuck on at a stiff angle to their necks. Oryx, handsome big buck with black markings on their grey bodies and long straight horns—beautiful beasts. Ostriches of course, silly haughty birds evidently anxious to rank as animals and jeered at by birds because they cannot fly. . . . So remote were we from war and thoughts of war in this land of peace and sunshine that the only possibility of disturbance was conveyed on a Government notice board close by: '*Fishermen, beware of rhinos here*'.

On 8th January 1941, while the Second World War was raging, B-P died peacefully and happily, and was laid to rest in the little cemetery at Nyeri, a few hundred yards from his little home 'Paxtu'.

Mount Kenya, which he had loved to watch from his balcony was shrouded in grey mist when the long procession of mourners, moving in slow step to the beat of muffled drums, approached the cemetery while the minute gun crashed forth its farewell.

Sailors, soldiers, civilians—representatives of all communities in Kenya—walked in the procession, headed by the Governor and the General Officer Commanding the Troops, and the Scout Commissioner led a mixed assembly of European, Asian and African Scouts, typifying his two lives of service.

At the graveside, too, with their President, was a group of Guides and Brownies.

So the Founder was borne to his last resting-place on the green hillside facing the mountain that he knew in its every mood. As the moving service ended the sun came out and as the procession left the grave-side the peak of the mountain was shining in a clear blue sky.

*   *   *

The Scouts have a sign—a dot within a circle—used in wide games and tracking expeditions to signify to their fellow Scouts who are following that they have gone home.

This sign appeared now not only beside a grave in Nyeri but on thousands of Memorial Service papers throughout the world. A truly great Scout had gone home.

His memorial stands today in Westminster Abbey in the heart of the city in which he was born, but his continuing living memorial remains in those millions of Scouts and Guides in whatever part of the world they may be, who have been and are the proud and happy members of the Movements he founded.

Pax

Few pioneers live long enough to see what they have done. Most men are glad if they can leave the world a single son. Did ever man, before he died, see such a dream come true? Did any leave so many living monuments as you?

A. P. H.
(Alan Percival Herbert)

APPENDIX I

A FAREWELL NOTE TO MY BROTHER SCOUTERS
AND TO GUIDERS

(Found after B-P's death)

Cecil Rhodes said at the end of his life (and I, in my turn, feel the truth of it), 'So much to do and so little time to do it'.

No-one can hope to see the consummation, as well as the start, of a big venture within the short span of one life-time.

I have had an extraordinary experience in seeing the development of Scouting from its beginning up to its present stage.

But there is a vast job before it. The Movement is only now getting into its stride.

(When I speak of Scouting I include in it Guiding also.)

The one part which I can claim as mine towards promoting the Movement is that I have been lucky enough to find you men and women to form a group of the right stamp which can be relied upon to carry it to its goal.

You will do well to keep your eyes open, in your turn, for worthy successors to whom you can, with confidence, hand on the torch.

Don't let it become a salaried organisation: keep it a voluntary Movement of patriotic service.

The Movement has already, in the comparatively short period of its existence, established itself onto a wide and so strong a footing as to show most encouraging promise of what may be possible to it in the coming years.

Its aim is to produce healthy, happy, helpful citizens, of both sexes, to eradicate the prevailing narrow self-interest, personal, political, sectarian and national, and to substitute for it a broader spirit of self-sacrifice and service in the cause of humanity; and thus to develop mutual goodwill and co-operation not only within our own country but abroad between all countries. Experience shows that this consummation is no idle or fantastic dream, but is a practical possibility—if we work for it; and it means, when attained, peace, prosperity and happiness for all.

The 'encouraging promise' lies in the fact that the hundreds of thousands of boys and girls who are learning our ideals today, will be the fathers and mothers of millions in the near future, in whom they will in turn inculcate the same ideals—PROVIDED THAT THESE ARE REALLY AND UNMISTAKABLY IMPRESSED UPON THEM BY THEIR LEADERS OF TODAY.

Therefore, you who are Scouters and Guiders are not only doing a great work for your neighbours' children but are also helping in practical fashion to bring to pass God's Kingdom of peace and goodwill upon earth. So from my heart I wish you God-speed in your effort.

Robert Baden-Powell

APPENDIX II

B-P'S MEDALS AND DECORATIONS

These decorations and many other articles presented to Lord Baden-Powell may be seen, free of charge, at Baden-Powell House, Queen's Gate, London, SW7 5JS

Ashanti Star Medal	1895
Matabele Campaign Medal	1896-7
South African War Queen's Medal	1899
South African War King's Medal	1900
Companion Order of the Bath	1901
Knight Commander of the Order of the Bath	1909
Knight Commander of the Victorian Order	1909
Chilean Order of Merit	1910
Coronation Medal (King George V)	1911
Knight of Grace of St. John of Jerusalem	1912
Knight Grand Cross of Alphonso XII (Spain)	1919
Grand Commander of the Order of Christ (Portugal)	1920
Grand Commander of the Order of the Redeemer (Greece)	1920
Baronetcy	1921
Storkos of the Order of Dannebrog (Denmark)	1921
Order of the Commander of the Crown (Belgium)	1921
Commander of the Legion of Honour (France)	1922
Grand Cross of the Victorian Order	1923
Order of Polonia Restituta (Poland)	1927
Knight Grand Cross of Order of St. Michael and St. George	1928
Order of Amanullah (Afghanistan)	1928
Order of Merit, First Class (Hungary)	1929
Order of the White Lion (Czechoslovakia)	1929
Order of the Phoenex (Greece)	1929

Peerage	1929
Grand Cross of the Order of Merit (Austria) . .	1931
Grand Cross of Gediminus (Lithuania) . . .	1932
Grand Cross of Orange of Nassau (Holland) . .	1932
Commander of the Order of the Oak of Luxembourg .	1932
Red Cross of Estonia	1933
Grand Cross of the Order of the Sword (Sweden) .	1933
Grand Cross of the Three Stars (Latvia) . .	1933
Jubilee Medal (George V)	1935
Grand Cordon of Legion of Honour . . .	1936
Order of Merit	1937
Coronation Medal (George VI)	1937

FREEDOMS:

Cities of Newcastle on Tyne, Bangor, Cardiff, Hawick, Kingston on Thames (1913), Guildford (1928), Poole (1929), Blandford (1929), LONDON (1929), Canterbury (1930), Pontefract (1933).

HON. DEGREES:

Doctor of Law Edinburgh (1910)
Doctor Toronto University (1923)
Doctor McGill University, Montreal (1923)
Doctor of Civil Law (DCL) Oxford University (1923)
LLD Liverpool University (1929)
LLD Cambridge University (1931)

APPENDIX III
B-P'S PUBLISHED WORKS

1884   *Reconnaissance and Scouting* William Clowes & Sons Ltd

1885   *Cavalry Instruction* Harrison & Sons

1889   *Pigsticking and Hoghunting* Harrison & Sons

1896   *The Downfall of Prempeh* Methuen

1897   *The Matabele Campaign* Methuen

1899   *Aids to Scouting for NCO's and Men* Gale & Polden

1900   *Sport in War* Heinemann

1901   *Notes and Instructions for the South African Constabulary* (Booklet)

1907   *Sketches in Mafeking and East Africa* Smith Elder & Co.

1908   *Scouting for Boys* (In six fortnightly parts) C. Arthur Pearson

         Scouting for Boys (Complete Edition) C. Arthur Pearson

1909   *Yarns for Boy Scouts* C. Arthur Pearson

1910   *Scouting Games* C. Arthur Pearson

1912   *Handbook for Girl Guides* (In collaboration with Miss Agnes Baden-Powell) C. Arthur Pearson

1913   *Boy Scouts Beyond the Seas* C. Arthur Pearson

1914   *Quick Training for War* Gale & Polden

1915   *Indian Memories* Herbert Jenkins

         My Adventures as a Spy C. Arthur Pearson

1916   *Young Knights of the Empire* C. Arthur Pearson

         The Wolf Cub's Handbook C. Arthur Pearson

1918   *Girl Guiding* C. Arthur Pearson

1919   *Aids to Scoutmastership* Herbert Jenkins

1921   *What Scouts Can Do* C. Arthur Pearson

         An Old Wolf's Favourites C. Arthur Pearson

1922   *Rovering to Success* Herbert Jenkins

1927   *Life's Snags and How to Meet Them* C. Arthur Pearson

1929   *Scouting and Youth Movements* Ernest Benn

1933   *Lessons from the Varsity of Life* C. Arthur Pearson
1934   *Adventures and Accidents* Methuen
1935   *Scouting Round the World* Herbert Jenkins
1936   *Adventuring to Manhood* C. Arthur Pearson
1937   *African Adventures* C. Arthur Pearson
1938   *Birds and Beasts of Africa* Macmillan
1939   *Paddle Your Own Canoe* Macmillan
1940   *More Sketches of Kenya* Macmillan

Index